*Refiguring* ENGLISH STUDIES

Refiguring Englisl scholarship on En… profession, and a vocation. To that end, the series publishes historical work that considers the ways in which English studies has constructed itself and its objects of study; investigations of the relationships among its constituent parts as conceived in both disciplinary and institutional terms; and examinations of the role the discipline has played or should play in the larger society and public policy. In addition, the series seeks to feature studies which, by their form or focus, challenge our notions about how the written "work" of English can or should be done; and to feature writings that represent the professional lives of the discipline's members in both traditional and nontraditional settings. The series also includes scholarship that considers the discipline's possible futures or that draws upon work in other disciplines to shed light on developments in English studies.



**Volumes in the Series**

Bruce McComiskey, editor, *English Studies Reimagined: A New Context for Linguistics, Rhetoric and Composition, Creative Writing, Literature, Cultural Studies, and English Education* (2022)

Laurie Grobman and Joyce Kinkead, *Undergraduate Research in English Studies* (2010)

John A. Staunton, *Deranging English/Education: Teacher Inquiry, Literary Studies, and Hybrid Visions of "English" for 21st Century Schools* (2008)

Laurie Grobman, *Multicultural Hybridity: Transforming American Literary Scholarship and Pedagogy* (2007)

Linda S. Bergmann and Edith M. Baker, editors, *Composition and/or Literature: The End(s) of Education* (2006)

Bruce McComiskey, editor, *English Studies: An Introduction to the Discipline(s)* (2006)

Ray Misson and Wendy Morgan, *Critical Literacy and the Aesthetic: Transforming the English Classroom* (2006)

Shari J. Stenberg, *Professing and Pedagogy: Learning the Teaching of English* (2005)

Chris W. Gallagher, *Radical Departures: Composition and Progressive Pedagogy* (2002)

Robert P. Yagelski and Scott A. Leonard, *The Relevance of English: Teaching That Matters in Students' Lives* (2002)

Derek Owens, *Composition and Sustainability: Teaching for a Threatened Generation* (2001)

Charles M. Anderson and Marian M. MacCurdy, editors, *Writing and Healing: Toward an Informed Practice* (2000)

Anne J. Herrington and Marcia Curtis, *Persons in Process: Four Stories of Writing and Personal Development in College* (2000)

Amy Lee, *Composing Critical Pedagogies: Teaching Writing as Revision* (2000)

Stephen M. North, with Barbara A. Chepaitis, David Coogan, Lâle Davidson, Ron MacLean, Cindy L. Parrish, Jonathan Post, and Beth Weatherby, *Refiguring the Ph.D. in English Studies: Writing, Doctoral Education, and the Fusion-Based Curriculum* (2000)

Stephen Parks, *Class Politics: The Movement for the Students' Right to Their Own Language* (2000)

Michael Blitz and C. Mark Hurlbert, *Letters for the Living: Teaching Writing in a Violent Age* (1998)

Bruce Horner and Min-Zhan Lu, *Representing the "Other": Basic Writers and the Teaching of Basic Writing* (1998)

Jane Maher, *Mina P. Shaughnessy: Her Life and Work* (1997)

James A. Berlin, *Rhetorics, Poetics, and Cultures: Refiguring College English Studies* (1996)

Robin Varnum, *Fencing with Words: A History of Writing Instruction at Amherst College during the Era of Theodore Baird, 1938–1966* (1996)

Jed Rasula, *The American Poetry Wax Museum: Reality Effects, 1940–1990* (1995)

David B. Downing, editor, *Changing Classroom Practices: Resources for Literary and Cultural Studies* (1994)

# *English Studies Reimagined*

## *A New Context for Linguistics, Rhetoric and Composition, Creative Writing, Literature, Cultural Studies, and English Education*

Edited by

Bruce McComiskey

NCTE

National Council of Teachers of English
340 N. Neil St., Suite #104, Champaign, IL 61820
www.ncte.org

Staff Editor: Bonny Graham
Manuscript Editor: Michael Ryan
Interior Design: Jenny Jensen Greenleaf
Cover Design: Pat Mayer
Cover Image: iStock.com/filo
NCTE Stock Number: 15411; eStock Number: 15435
ISBN 978-0-8141-1541-1; eISBN 978-0-8141-1543-5
ISSN 1073-9637



It is the policy of NCTE in its journals and other publications to provide a forum for the open discussion of ideas concerning the content and the teaching of English and the language arts. Publicity accorded to any particular point of view does not imply endorsement by the Executive Committee, the Board of Directors, or the membership at large, except in announcements of policy, where such endorsement is clearly specified.

NCTE provides equal employment opportunity (EEO) to all staff members and applicants for employment without regard to race, color, religion, sex, national origin, age, physical, mental or perceived handicap/disability, sexual orientation including gender identity or expression, ancestry, genetic information, marital status, military status, unfavorable discharge from military service, pregnancy, citizenship status, personal appearance, matriculation or political affiliation, or any other protected status under applicable federal, state, and local laws.

Every effort has been made to provide current URLs and email addresses, but because of the rapidly changing nature of the web, some sites and addresses may no longer be accessible.

**Library of Congress Cataloging-in-Publication Data**

Names: McComiskey, Bruce, 1963- editor.
Title: English studies reimagined : a new context for linguistics, rhetoric and composition, creative writing, literature, cultural studies, and English education / edited by Bruce McComiskey.
Description: Champaign, Illinois : National Council of Teachers of English, [2022] | Series: Refiguring English studies, 1073-9637 ; 23 | Includes bibliographical references and index. | Summary: "Explores the need for a shift in the discipline of English studies from a national to a global orientation to remain relevant in the new century, focusing on the subdisciplines of linguistics, rhetoric and composition, literature and literary criticism, critical theory and cultural studies, English education, and creative writing"—Provided by publisher.
Identifiers: LCCN 2021047245 (print) | LCCN 2021047246 (ebook) | ISBN 9780814115411 (trade paperback) | ISBN 9780814115435 (adobe pdf)
Subjects: LCSH: English philology—Study and teaching—United States. | Education and globalization—United States.
Classification: LCC PE68.U5 E59 2022 (print) | LCC PE68.U5 (ebook) | DDC 420.71/073—dc23/eng/20211222
LC record available at https://lccn.loc.gov/2021047245
LC ebook record available at https://lccn.loc.gov/2021047246

*For Helena*

# CONTENTS

# Introduction

Bruce McComiskey
*Virginia Tech University*

If you ask an English professor, "What is English studies?" you'll likely be met with a frustrated grunt and a muttered, "Oh, yikes," or an honest, "I've spent the last twenty years trying to figure that out." The fact is, English studies can't be boiled down to a one-word definition (grammar, writing, literature, theory, or teaching). It is the complex integration of several different disciplines that all, in their own ways, contribute to a larger project: the analysis, critique, and production of discourse in social context.

There are many different ways to talk about English studies as a complex and integrated subject. In this introduction, I focus on two foundational concepts, *nationalism* and *difference*, and each subsequent chapter carries the theme of difference (and sometimes nationalism) throughout the rest of the book. Nationalism and difference have never coexisted comfortably, yet their dissonant relationship has shaped the structures (curriculum, pedagogy, canon) and methods (analysis, critique, production) that have characterized English studies from its beginnings to the present.

The history of many aspects of modern English studies extends as far back as Classical civilization; however, what we now recognize as the academic discipline and university subject of English actually emerged from nationalist fervor following World War I. This early twentieth-century nationalism provided fertile ideological ground for the hegemony of British and American literature in English studies, and English's legitimating relationship with nationalist ideologies intensified after World War II. Although literature and literary criticism rode the wave of postwar nationalism to a place of prominence in English studies, linguistics, rhetoric and composition, creative writing, critical theory and cultural studies, and English education were also significantly influenced by nationalist ideologies.

Certain manifestations of nationalism, such as patriotism, often represent positive practices based on nonexclusionary beliefs, adaptable to many circumstances. However, like any ideology, nationalism can become overly rigid and simplified, unable to respond to the evolving contextual pressures of a changing world. Rigid and simplified nationalism can turn ugly, as it has in the United States and Europe during the past decade or so. This raw underbelly of nationalism breeds contempt for difference, fear of diversity, resentment of multiculturalism, disdain for globalization, and condescension toward cosmopolitanism. Nationalism's recent exclusionary beliefs and practices have become so rigid and simplified that they can no longer adapt to new cultural and social circumstances, leaving English studies (including all of its students, teachers, writers, scholars, and administrators) with some hard decisions to make about the relationship between its past and its present and future. If English studies stands stubbornly on an ideological foundation of nationalism without evolving in response to the recent moral disintegration of this ideology, then English studies will become a petrified or zombified discourse.

All discourses are historically situated and socially contextual, and these situations and contexts constantly evolve over time. Successful discourses, which are more process than structure, adapt (or are adapted by their practitioners) to evolving circumstances. Unsuccessful discourses persist unchanged despite increasingly unsupportive contexts that make static discourses archaic, obsolete, and irrelevant. These unsuccessful discourses fail precisely because they become petrified or zombified, organically dead, giving only the appearance of life. In *One-Dimensional Man*, Herbert Marcuse calls discourses like Marxism "petrified" because they have not adapted to the new context of advanced technology. Petrified discourses are so rigid, simplified, and closed in their languages and ideologies that they are no longer relevant. In *Power in the Global Age*, Ulrich Beck calls late capitalism, objective science, and exclusionary nationalism "zombie" discourses because they have not adapted to the new context of a global economy.

Zombie discourses devour living discourses without direction or discrimination, guided by a purpose of destruction.

The social contexts in which English studies finds itself have evolved in the twenty-first century, both away from nationalism and toward globalization, cosmopolitanism, and planetarity. And the discourses of English must evolve (or continue to evolve) with the pressures and constraints of those contexts if they wish to remain significant and relevant. But discourses do not evolve on their own with some invisible ideological engine driving change. Students, teachers, writers, scholars, and administrators within English studies will all have to work together—consciously and actively—in order to influence the course of discursive change in English studies. We will choose our own fate, whether we are statues of stone (petrified), the living dead (zombified), or relevant humanists.

The chapters throughout this book offer difference as an alternative discourse to the rigid and simplified nationalist discourses that have structured English studies in the past. While some English departments have already pushed their courses and curricula beyond the stifling discourses of nationalism and into the progressive discourses of difference (emphasizing sociolinguistics, comparative literature, cultural studies, and critical pedagogy, for example), many are still mired in stale requirements covering historical periods and nationalist identities. This book, *English Studies Reimagined: A New Context for Linguistics, Rhetoric and Composition, Creative Writing, Literature, Cultural Studies, and English Education*, seeks to reinforce existing reforms in progressive English departments and to encourage self-conscious reflection and change in stagnant English departments. Such a purpose (of reinforcing and encouraging change) requires deep engagement from multiple communities within English studies, including students, teachers, writers, scholars, and administrators.

Since its purpose is complex, *English Studies Reimagined* addresses varied and complex audiences. We have composed this book for English majors in introductory or capstone courses, making the content and structure of difference in English accessible to future practitioners of the discipline. We have composed this book for graduate students who want a more detailed understanding of the entire scope of English studies, perhaps with the purpose of choosing an emphasis. We have composed this book for teachers, writers, and scholars who seek points of intersection among the disciplines that make up English studies, reinforcing a common interest in the theme of difference. And we have composed this book for administrators who evaluate the work of English studies practitioners without specialized knowledge of the entire scope of the discipline and all of its moving parts.

## Historical Context

The earliest histories of the disciplines we now associate with English studies extend all the way back to the Classical liberal arts of grammar, dialectic, and rhetoric, which were later formalized into the *trivium* during the early Middle Ages. The trivium remained the model of liberal arts education and the structure of curriculum in Europe and the United States through the early nineteenth century. The liberal arts universities that were established under the influence of the trivium employed humanistic curricula to prepare prominent citizens from elite families for civic leadership roles in politics, law, and religion. These curricula emphasized the integration of knowledge, the ethical foundation of human action, and the reinforcement of traditional wisdom. Regarding the language arts, students in these universities translated important Greek and Latin texts, composed hortatory fables and histories, argued theses about controversial issues, persuaded audiences to take ethical action, and judged the style and substance of culturally salient texts, among many other things. Universities following this liberal arts model dotted the European landscape from the early Middle Ages through the nineteenth century, and they emerged in the new republic, the United States, during and after the Enlightenment.

Throughout the nineteenth century, the United States witnessed advances in manufacturing and communication technologies that transformed the base of the economy and resulted in massive population shifts from rural agrarian communities to rapidly growing cities. The United States soon experienced an infrastructural crisis, with sparsely populated rural land that was left unproductive and densely populated urban sprawl that was unsanitary, uncivil, and unsafe. Everyone recognized the problems, but no one knew how to solve them. The country's only educated citizens, trained in the liberal arts, could argue for sanitation, but they could not engineer sewers; they could praise civil society, but they could not design spaces for citizens to engage in civil debate; they could describe fertile landscapes, but they could not grow food, mine minerals, or harvest timber; and they could illustrate the power and safety of structures around the world, but they could not construct buildings to stand for generations.

In order to address the social and material problems associated with this infrastructural crisis, the thirty-seventh Congress passed the Morrill Act of 1862, which Abraham Lincoln signed into law one year after the beginning of the Civil War and one year before he signed the Emancipation Proclamation.[1] By the late nineteenth century, especially in the United States, public, state-funded universities emerged rapidly from the land and money provided to states through the Morrill Act. These new so-called "land grant" universities were modeled after German research universities, which emphasized objective science over dogmatic religion, discovery of new knowledge over the conservation of traditional wisdom, and disciplinary specialization over practical integration. More specifically, these research universities privileged science, math, farming, mining, and engineering, not the liberal arts, which remained the province of small, elite colleges.

The proliferation of research universities in the United States during the late nineteenth century caused a shift in college curricula away from the liberal arts and toward the objective sciences. Rhetoric, which functioned as the capstone of liberal arts education before the Morrill Act, had lost its usefulness in the rapidly emerging German-style research universities. What these new universities needed was instruction in basic literacy skills, not stylistic flourishes; clarity in speaking, not passionate delivery; and fixed expository structures, not situational persuasive appeals. In just a few decades, rhetoric became composition, and the primary function of composition was to serve the literacy needs of the research university, not the rhetorical needs of its surrounding community.

Out of all the disciplines that had thrived in the trivium before the Morrill Act, only one, philology (the scientific analysis of historical language change, which was part of *grammar* in the trivium), survived this shift as the paradigm-discipline of English studies. All other disciplines in English studies participated far too much in epistemological relativism to acquire any significant credibility in the new nineteenth-century research universities. Philology was a distinctly German (thus, objective and methodical) approach to historical linguistics, and its scholarly goal was the *complete* understanding of language change from its origin in Proto-Indo-European to its pinnacle in the Renaissance. For philologists, literary texts were not objects of aesthetic criticism but simply the best-preserved examples of language in every historical period.

Most of the professors of philology in United States English departments around the first decade of the twentieth century had actually been educated in Germany. However, this academic love affair with German education in general, and Germanic philology in particular, would end soon enough, strained by the national alliances and divisions created in the political conflicts of World War I.[2] Germany was our military enemy, and the ethos and pathos that defined Germany in opposition to the United States and its allies led to a general distrust of Germanic methods in many United States universities, opening a path for the liberal arts (and for literature in particular) to seize disciplinary control from philology. Thus, the discipline we now know as English studies really took on its present characteristics after World War I, following the rejection in Britain and the United States of Germans, Germany, and all things Germanic.[3]

After World War I, Britain and the United States experienced a sharp rise in personal and public commitment to nationalist ideologies. Writing in 1930, just twelve years after the end of World War I, S. Gale Lowrie declared that "[n]ationalism is the most important issue in world politics today" (35). And in 1934, just sixteen years after the war, James C. King noted that "the postwar period has seen the steady growth of nationalism not only in the political but in the cultural and economic spheres" (819). The rise of nationalism throughout these early decades of the twentieth century legitimated the study of British and American literatures (at least in Britain and the United States) since these national literatures represented and reinforced the values of bourgeoning nationalist sentiments in those countries.

During this time, English education (the university subject of teaching English from kindergarten through high school), according to Jory Brass, "played a central role . . . in modern nation-building by fostering youths' self-disciplinary capacities and attuning them to norms of individual and national identity. . . . In the United States, these practices of modern governance have been connected to constructions of 'America' that are not primarily geographical, but constituted in discourses" (41). Although the research universities established by the Morrill Act of 1862 responded in progressive ways to the infrastructural crises of the nineteenth century, English education responded in conservative ways. Brass writes, "English teaching was named an important means to constitute a particular kind of 'America' (and 'American') in response to a series of fears linked to urbanization, industrialization, the perceived decline of Christianity, and demographic changes brought about by the migration of southern blacks and influxes of immigrants from southern and eastern Europe" (41). The main problem was that African Americans and European immigrants considered their identities to be centered in local communities, not national imaginaries. According to Brass, one critical function of early English education was "to displace youths' connections to local community and place in order to establish racial and national imaginaries as dominant forms of belonging" (42). These racial and national imaginaries were structured hierarchically. For Brass, the "nation-building project" of English education "deployed hierarchical constructions of difference that divided the world by race and nation" and "identified the country's increasingly heterogeneous population as a threat to national identity and the national tongue" (47).

As a countermeasure to the perceived increase in cultural and racial heterogeneity, English education emphasized prescriptive grammar and literary education as a strategy for establishing a dominant discourse in which difference is irrational and un-American. Brass writes, "Other nations, races, and languages were located outside of rationality," and these *others* "were positioned as foreign or subaltern groups outside of constructions of America, even as they had inhabited the nation's geographical borders for generations" (48). To stop the imposition of other cultures on traditional American values, English education employed grammar and literature as tools to shape young minds. Brass writes, "[N]ational ideals and consciousness were largely dependent upon the establishment of a common tongue and of shared experiences constituted by literary texts. . . . Uniting nationality and universality, English teachers saw themselves as saving youth from the parochial, irrational, and corrupting influences of their social environments" (51–52). Before and after World War I, English education held fast to its values of homogeneity and nationalism and the propagation of these values through instruction in grammar and literature. These values were also well represented in university education more generally at the time, which caused a crisis of legitimation for philology.

By the 1920s and 1930s, philology had become an ideologically problematic discourse in the United States and Britain, embodying Germanic characteristics in a new context of strengthening pro-Anglo and anti-Germanic nationalisms. Philologists during this time had three choices in order to avoid petrification, zombification, and extinction altogether: either philologists seceded from English studies and joined departments of anthropology (a social science), where it evolved into the translation and analysis of indigenous languages; or philologists remained in departments of English (a liberal art) and retooled their subject into the humanistic (not scientific) study of early British and Northern European languages and literatures; or philologists remained in English departments and reframed the study of historical language change into structural linguistics, which supplemented the analysis of literary stylistics and the teaching of composition. Each of these choices washed away many of the Germanic qualities that caused philology to be devalued after World War I, breathing new life into a discipline that could have vanished from United States and British university curricula without so much as a whimper. As an ideological (not just intellectual) enterprise, philology adapted to its evolving contexts and has consequently survived, even thrived.

British literature had little work to do in order to gain credibility as a subject for university study early in the twentieth century since its predecessor, philology, had given the analysis of Anglo-Saxon languages and literatures academic credibility before World War I. Since philology examined only older texts, rarely extending its interests past Shakespeare, it supported British literature as an object of academic study but did not support American literature, which emerged too late to benefit from the ideological remains of scientific philology. Instead, American literature was viewed as popular culture, not a legitimate object of study for a serious academic discipline. Elizabeth Renker writes, "Because it represented a complete severance of literature from philology, American literature represented a challenge to the scientific foundations of professionalization on which 'English' as a university subject had built its prestige" (350).

Fortunately for English studies (and especially for American literature) in the United States, World War I would turn things around. Christopher Clausen writes, "the First World War gave American cultural nationalism a sharper edge" (66), and Renker explains the impact of this sharper edge on American literary studies:

> America's place on the battlefield was in fact a great boon for American literature's professional fortunes. The surge of nationalism produced by the Great War fostered an interest in America's literature both here and abroad. . . . The powerful force of nationalism unleashed by the Great War was ready ammunition for the American literature scholars in America who were still seeking gains in the academy. . . . The field achieved institutional maturity during this period not through a simple evolutionary process in which the war was an accidental factor, but because the phenomenon of the war produced cultural effects that erased the early image of femininity that clung to American literature. . . . In the cyclical process of institutionalization, war replaced science as the agent of legitimation. American literature may have been scientifically, historically, and aesthetically thin, but once recuperated by nationalistic trends set in motion by the two world wars, it could no longer be dismissed as an "inferior" project. Instead, it became a literature of "democratic citizenship" that burgeoned with influence and importance in a new world order. (357–59)

After World War I, in addition to science and technology, nationalism also became an important legitimating force in research universities, and this trend toward nationalism in Britain and the United States would redouble after World War II.

The discrediting of Germanic philology in English studies left a wide range of British and especially American literatures unexamined, and literary critics filled that void. These critics rejected philology's orientation toward literature as examples of historical language change and instead valued these texts as aesthetic objects, eventually creating through their scholarship a canon of imaginative works that could "stand the test of time." Since these critics were generally white, affluent men living in the United States and Britain, they tended to value literature that had been written by and represented the social and cultural values of white, affluent men living in the United States and Britain. These values, though clearly situated, were presented in critical writing as if they were universal. The socially elite and culturally Anglo literatures that passed as representations of universal values in the emerging literary canon excluded texts that did not embody these values. The obvious problem for African American writers during the 1930s and 1940s (and still today) was that their own nationalist values were different from the American (i.e., white, male, affluent) values made to seem universal by the legitimating hegemony of the literary canon and the literary criticism that created and reinforced it.

In 1937, Richard Wright explained that "the nationalist character of the Negro people is unmistakable. Psychologically this nationalism is reflected in the whole of Negro culture, and especially in folklore" (100). Later, Wright continued,

> The nationalist aspects of Negro life are as sharply manifest in the social institutions of Negro people as in folklore. There is a Negro church, a Negro press, a Negro social world, a Negro sporting world, a Negro business world, a Negro school system, Negro professions; in short, a Negro way of life in America. The Negro people did not ask for this, and deep down, though they express themselves through their institutions and adhere to this special way of life, they do not want it now. This special existence was forced upon them from without by lynch rope, bayonet, and mob rule. (100)

African American nationalism in the 1930s and after is defined as different from the white, male, affluent American nationalism that supplied the literary canon with its foundation of seemingly universal values. African American writers, representing their own nationalist values in their writing, were excluded from the emerging canon and thus also from publishing companies and universities.

Whereas the white, male, affluent canon paraded its values as universal, African American writers situated their own nationalism in the dialectical interaction between personal experience and larger social movements. Wright explains, "[A] nationalist spirit in Negro writing means a nationalism carrying the highest possible pitch of social consciousness. . . . For purposes of creative expression, it means that the Negro writer must realize within the area of his own personal experience those impulses which, when prefigured in terms of broad social movements, constitute the stuff of nationalism" (101). The situated nationalist values of the white, male, affluent canon posed as universal, but the nationalist values of African American writers in the decades before and after World War II were viewed as blatantly situated, overtly contextual, and thus not universal. This sense of non-universality in African American nationalism both resulted from and caused feelings of isolation among African American writers from the broader American culture. Wright explains, "Barred for decades from the theater and publishing houses, Negro writers have been *made* to feel a sense of difference. So deep has this white-hot iron of exclusion been burnt into their hearts that thousands have all but lost the desire to become identified with American civilization" (106). For Wright, the answer lies in African American writers' identification with other disenfranchised peoples, not with the dominant American culture that actively excludes them. Wright explains, "Perspective for Negro writers will come when they have looked and brooded so hard and long upon the harsh lot of their race and compared it with the hopes and struggles of minority peoples everywhere that the cold facts have begun to tell them something" (104). For African American writers, nationalism, especially literary nationalism, was (and still is) a source of oppression, not liberation.

Literature was not the only discipline housed in English that was caught up in the fervor of postwar nationalism and infused with white, male, and affluent values. Structural linguistics, too, was so much associated with the United States before the 1960s that it was often called American linguistics, and structural linguistics served the larger project of American nationalism very well. Andrew Linn writes, for example, that early American structural linguistics assumed "some sort of natural relationship between a people and their language, and indeed the perceived link between language and nation, for better or worse, remains a strong one" (359–60). Just as the literary canon limits variation in its drive toward cultural uniformity, so too did early structural linguistics deny variation and marginalize difference, supporting the values of white, male, affluent linguists. In 1967, Dell Hymes explained,

> Structural linguistics was conceived as a discipline which concerned itself little, if at all, with society. Its province was rather to analyze those aspects of language which belonged to the realm of form as such. There was little need to ask questions which demanded a more intimate knowledge of users of a language, speech acts, and speech communities, than could be assumed on the basis of common experience or common assumption. The whole temper of linguistics was impersonal and formal to a degree. In the earlier period of the American science, it seemed indeed almost intellectually indecent, or wrong in principle, to obtrude observations that smacked of heterogeneity in descriptive result, through appeal to the users and uses of a language. The assumption was that in some way not in the least clearly defined as to method it was possible for the linguist to arrive at conclusive statements which would hold for a given "language" and its entire community as such. One was rarely in a position to say whether such an inclusive analysis reflected in fact a particular informant, perhaps a particular type of context, topic, or style, or was a carefully tested generalization from study of a full range of users and occasions of use. (632–33)

Linn and Hymes would both agree that structural linguistics' disengagement from society actually serves to protect and preserve a certain segment of that society (white, affluent men) from the threat of variation and difference. In order to preserve the nationalist values that grounded the universal analysis of language, structural linguistics established separate subfields, such as dialect and idiolect studies, that would account for linguistic variation and difference without threatening the universal coherence of structural linguistics.

Structural linguistics, literature, and English education would continue their reliance on nationalism as a legitimating ideology well past World War II, even persisting into the present day. Although other disciplines in English studies had more complicated relationships with nationalism, it is nevertheless important to recognize that nationalism retained at least an indirect influence on all of the disciplines in English studies. The nationalist hegemony of American structural linguistics and British and American literatures exerted a constant force on disciplinary values and curricula in English departments. In rhetoric and composition, for example, first-year composition classes often used British and American literature as their content and resorted to prescriptive grammar as their method. Thus, the universalist sense of language structure gained from prescriptive grammar was joined ineluctably with the nationalist values propagated through literary studies. Anne Ruggles Gere explains that

> World War I led to many realignments in education, and approaches to the teaching of writing were among them. The war-induced need to develop a stronger sense of national pride and loyalty caused a major shift in English studies. The dominance of British literature in the curriculum was supplanted by an increased attention to American authors as a way of fostering a greater sense of national pride in students. In a general way, composition became linked to the process of affirming nationhood, but writing instructors did not uniformly embrace this idea. (102)

One of the reasons for composition's partial alignment with American nationalism was its continued association with literature as the content of writing courses. However, while literature did supply the content for these early composition courses, the function of literary texts within composition was more deliberately subjectivist than nationalist, a means to develop personal voice and creative expression, and not exclusively as a means to learn or express nationalist values.

Like composition, creative writing also adopted a complex relationship to the nationalism that grounded most of English studies, emphasizing personal expression in style and a generalized sense of craft in method. Because style and craft do not directly reflect nationalist values, creative writing was only indirectly influenced by the nationalist values that were inherent in the literary canon. The examples of style and craft that were assigned in creative writing workshops following World War II came mostly from *modern* American literature, which at times even challenged traditional literary values. Also, in a much more conscious and direct way, creative writing rejected nationalism as a constraint on creative expression. D. G. Myers writes, "If a man hoped to develop himself as a creative artist, he had to break with business and the institutions of American culture" (83).

The purpose of creative writing in these early workshop classes was to supplement the formal study of literature with what Myers calls a "constructivist" view, thus expanding and democratizing literary studies by emphasizing "the practical experience of writing" (8). Creative writing's constructivist view of literary studies sometimes challenged the established canon of historically significant works created through literary criticism, instead valuing modern American literary texts mainly as practical models of craft. But the more positive relationship between creative writing and literary criticism produced a kind of scholarship that enabled, as Myers points out, a "critical understanding conducted from within the conditions of literary practice" (133). The positive alliance between creative writing and constructivist criticism lent credibility to creative writing by association, and creative writing would soon take on additional curricular territory that had been neglected by composition. Throughout the 1940s and 1950s, as composition studies drifted more and more into basic skills courses in grammar and exposition, creative writing adopted composition's discarded modes, description and narration, emphasizing expression over explanation. For creative writing, these two associations (with criticism and composition) would prove fruitful, entrenching creative writing firmly in the ideal of progressive education that was changing the culture of universities throughout the United States, expanding its curricula and shifting academic values toward practice. However, while creative writing was thriving in public land grant universities (especially among white men), it remained absent from what would later be called Historically Black Colleges and Universities (HBCUs).

In his 1951 essay, "Creative Writing in the Negro College," published in the *Journal of Negro Education*, Philip Butcher writes, "creative writing is beginning to take its proper place in the curriculum as a legitimate and serious field of academic specialization" (160). However,

> [t]oo frequently the Negro college adopts the view that writing cannot be taught or is not worth teaching. The serious student with an insight into character and a flair for words gets little or no instruction in the procedure to be followed in submitting manuscripts to publishers, the current markets, editorial interests and prohibitions, agents, contracts, contests, writing workshops, the vogues in contemporary literature, and the techniques of his craft. His seed of interest and aptitude is not encouraged to take root. (160–61)

Since African American creative writers would most likely write about what they know—African American life and culture—it is a shame that HBCUs had been neglecting creative writing, since these universities are where many African American students would learn about their life and culture. Butcher continues, "The Negro writer should have the resources that the study of Negro history and literature can provide in terms of material for his writing. And he should have the objectivity, the emotional balance, and the sense of achievement and identity that he may gain from a knowledge of the role of the Negro and other minority groups in American culture" (161). In 1964, however, Saunders Redding, then professor of literature and creative writing at Hampton Institute, an HBCU founded in 1868, argues that the problem of African American writing is not one of identity (as Butcher suggests) but rather one of identification. In other words, Redding writes, for African American creative writers, "their *identity as Negroes* precludes their *identification with American writing*," and it "is immediately clear that this is something more than a 'literary' problem, a problem in writing" (58). Redding explains, "The Negro, and especially, later, the Negro writer, has always known who he is. . . . The Negro's identity was locked into the white man's fantasy construct of the slave, and Emancipation did not free him" (58). African American identity, especially in the 1960s, was clear enough and painful enough. The problem is that African American identity was refused the basic human right of identification with American life and values. Redding writes, "Although they are losing the power to annul the Negro's simple human dignity, white people retain the authority to disallow the Negro's participation in American civilization. Although whatever, besides his color, is distinctive about him was made so by the pressures of the American environment, he is not permitted his identification with American culture. He is kept outside it. As every-day citizen and as creative artists, he is relegated to a subculture and required to function within it" (61).

If American literature represents American values, then the inclusionary process of canonizing individual works by white, male, affluent authors involved, simultaneously, an exclusionary process of "the minimizing of Negro writing as projections of a significant aspect of American reality and a distinctive American experience" (Redding 62). This negative process of exclusion prevents African American creative writers from identifying with the very culture that oppresses them, and this exclusionary process preserves the purity and unity of "American" culture and the literature that embodies it. The fact is, identification would require white, male, affluent critics, builders of the canon, to recognize the raw underbelly of American nationalism and to negotiate a new ideological territory in which American nationalism could coexist with African American nationalism and other cultural identities and nationalisms that were emerging during the 1960s. Redding explains that African American creative writers "have come to know America, its flawed character and its bankrupt spirit, better than most Americans, but most Americans reject this special knowledge as disloyal and subversive, and Negro writers cannot even use it in recreating the reality of their experiences, their world" (66). For African American creative writers, from Wright to Butcher to Redding to writers in the present day, identification is the problem, not identity. If African American creative writers refuse to identify with a morally corrupt culture that enslaved their ancestors and continues to disenfranchise them, then they are expelled from the legitimating institutions that enable literary success. And if African American creative writers attempt identification with this same American culture, then their writing is rejected as a corruption of "universal" (white, male, affluent) American values. This is now and always has been the dilemma for African American creative writers, and it is the same dilemma for all writers whose identities do not reflect white, male, affluent values.

The primarily African American civil rights movement of the 1960s morphed during the 1970s into a multicultural movement that would include other "non-white" identities, such as Asian American, Latin American, and, later, Native American. Chong Chon-Smith explains that Asian American literature experienced its birth in the context of a "multiethnic coalition" with African American publishers who did not share, and thus did not promote, the academic literary canon's white, male, affluent values (710). Under the term *non-white*, multiethnic literary coalitions across the country produced "literary works, critical journals, writers' organizations, publishing houses, festivals, and regional theaters" that transformed racial essentialism "into multiethnicity and interracial bonds" (711). While African American and Asian American authors struggled to get their work published in mainstream (white, male, affluent) venues, Native American authors experienced a more direct force of opposition. According to Kathleen Washburn, "Native Americans have long been the missing subjects of American literature, either excised from narratives of nation through colonial erasure or limited to the discourse of the 'vanishing Indian'" (380). Among Native American writers, tribal nationalism has historically been the ideological remedy to all-consuming American nationalism since Native American globalism or cosmopolitanism has always been met with colonization at best and obliteration at worst. By the 1980s, however, a new movement was afoot that would attempt to ease some of the pressures nationalism was exerting on identities of difference.

## Culture Wars

The dilemma of identity versus identification for African American, Asian American, Latin American, and Native American writers and scholars represents a larger crisis in American nationalism, and it highlights the problematic status of nationalism as an ideological foundation of English studies. According to Lloyd Kramer, like any idea that strives toward unification, nationalism "relies on unacknowledged sources or assumptions [and] represses issues or ideas or people that would call its assertions into question" (536). The nationalist narrative that still legitimates much (but not all) of English studies represses the memory of murdered Native Americans within the idealized myth of national emergence, suppresses the guilt of enslaving Africans and others in the name of national progress, and denies the influences of other nations on American writers and scholars through a critical process of dissociation. These critical acts of repression, suppression, and dissociation are the very genesis of nationalism in the first place, for without the constant presence of difference and conflict, there would be no need for unification. Kramer writes, "There would be no meaning in the search for unity within a nation or against other nations if the difference did not exist; nationalisms depend on difference" (537). This is the reason that nationalism in general, and the nationalist discourses that still structure curricula in English studies, are petrified and zombified, appearing to be animate when they are inanimate, consuming living discourses in a ravenous suppression of difference.

Since the narratives that construct nationalist discourses are themselves structured by the forces of absence and difference, their modernist ideological project can never be fully realized. Thus, Kramer concludes, "Recent discussions of the literary and linguistic construction of nationalism have therefore moved toward a 'multicultural' description of nations that focuses on the competing languages and narratives within a society" (537). While this is indeed a positive shift in our understanding of nationalist discourses, it has not fully penetrated the hard shell of English studies curriculum. Even where an African American literature class is required of all English majors, for example, this requirement simply creates an enclosed space for the discussion of African American nationalism separate from the canonical works that represent "American" (white, male, affluent) nationalism. This is clearly a strategy of control by means of isolation.

During the 1960s, some marginalized populations, like African Americans, women, and wage workers, began to push back against a unified nationalist ideology because they viewed it as a cause of their oppression, thus planting seeds of unrest that would evolve into the civil rights, women's liberation, and labor rights movements. Throughout these movements, there emerged a number of useful theories of oppression regarding race, gender, and class, and these theories began to make their way into academic institutions as critical perspectives and analytical methods. What emerged was a concern for *multiculturalism*, a blanket term for the study and critique of difference and oppression, and by the 1970s, English studies had received a much-needed injection of difference theory that continued to develop credibility, complexity, and efficacy through the end of the millennium. During this time, the world was becoming more globally oriented due to rapid advances in communication and travel technologies, providing a supportive context for English studies' newly emerging interest in multiculturalism as theory and method.

Although the world was becoming more and more global and cosmopolitan during the 1980s and 1990s, multiculturalism was fighting a difficult war of legitimation on two more-localized fronts. First, in English studies, the rise of multiculturalism during the 1980s and 1990s was viewed as a direct challenge to the nationalism that had given birth to the discipline in the first place. Second, the presidencies of Ronald Reagan (1981–1989) and George H. W. Bush (1989–1993) intensified nationalist sentiments in the United States, especially white nationalism.

According to Bethany Bryson, multiculturalism gained credibility in the academy generally because with it, "Students might become better prepared to operate in a global economy. They might develop more sophisticated cultural sensibilities, greater empathetic capacities, fewer prejudices, and more elastic intellectual abilities" (1–2). The discipline of English studies seemed best poised to accomplish these global goals, and linguistics, rhetoric and composition, creative writing, literature and literary criticism, critical theory and cultural studies, and English education seemed the best academic locations in which to foster empathy and acceptance. However, even during this furtive time for multiculturalism, not everyone in English studies was on board. According to Bryson, "Defenders of traditional education, on the other hand, saw the situation differently and worried that de-emphasizing Western culture might be dangerous. The ideas contained in those classic works of literature are, they argued, 'the glue that binds together our pluralistic nation'" (2).

So if literature actually serves to promote and maintain positive nationalist values, then the cultural diffusion of literature into non-nationalist difference and diversity may mean the disintegration of American and British nationalisms altogether, even their positive manifestations like patriotism. Bryson continues, "tinkering with culture could, indeed, be an easy way to change the world. But it could also be extremely dangerous—especially if it's *national* culture that we want to alter. If we change the culture too much, life as we know it could disappear. . . . The destruction of a value system can amount to the destruction of a nation" (7). Thus, defenders of traditional English curricula (which are still often divided into two nations and many periods) argue that "we should pay a lot more attention to culture, especially national culture and national values" (8). People on both sides of this debate, according to Bryson, "shared an extraordinary premise: that every time an English teacher put together a reading list, the future of a nation hung in the balance" (2).

Despite its potential for institutional reform (political, social, and academic), the popularity of multiculturalism in English studies has come and gone. Some battles were won, of course, but the war against nationalism as a legitimating discourse of English studies was lost. At the turn of the new millennium, multiculturalism had become a petrified and zombified discourse, giving the appearance of life despite the reality of death. Throughout the 1960s and 1970s, the difference theory that grounded multicultural practice in English studies had emerged organically from the grassroots activism of the civil rights, women's liberation, and labor rights movements. But by the 1980s, that foundation in social and political activism had given way to academic insularity in the isolated contexts of academic work. Scholars offering multicultural critiques of literature, or anything else, were entrenched in an educational system that employed them and valued their approaches so long as they did not dismantle the traditional values that maintained an English curriculum based on national and periodic divisions. Since multiculturalism did not at its heart challenge the nationalism (and its associated racism, sexism, and classism) that grounded English studies, it was easily co-opted in the service of this same nationalism.

Not only was multiculturalism co-opted by traditional nationalism in English studies, but also the more general ideological context of American culture and politics was moving steadily in the direction of white nationalism. According to Ronald Walters, one salient feature of the "Reagan Revolution" is "the extent to which the conservative ideology that fueled it has congealed into a nationalism in the United States" (141), a nationalism that harkens back to the pre-civil rights era. Walters writes,

> [T]he supporters of this nationalism have sounded a number of moral, social themes such as the preservation of the family, respect for law and order, anti-abortion, prayer in the schools, and others as a basis for restoring a pre-1960s social structure as the substance of "Americanness." They also attempted to repress public attention to and concern for the disadvantaged class—African Americans, other minorities, women, and others—in order to restore white dominance of the social order through the resurrection of the status of white men. (142)

Thus, Reagan and his conservative colleagues in Congress "shaped a vision of restructuring society, using the framework of a time which not only elevated the interest of the wealthy over the poor, but which also contained white hegemonic dominance" (142). One direct effect of these racist and sexist political policies was an "increase of incidents of racially motivated violence" (142) and a significant resurgence in membership and power among white nationalist groups like the Ku Klux Klan, the White Patriot Party, the Aryan Nations Church, and the World Aryan Congress (151).

This political and social restructuring that began during Reagan's presidency is a form of power that is dispersed across public institutions and is thus difficult to pin on any individual, but it is a power that is felt in very real ways by the individuals whose lives are directly subjected to it. In a strikingly frank passage written at the end of Reagan's second term, Walters summarizes his argument:

> [T]he current political culture contains a pervasive strain of white nationalism as one of its dynamic features. The origin of this nationalism was the reaction to movements for social change by African Americans, other disadvantaged groups, and youthful whites since World War II, which caused feelings of disempowerment by a segment of the white population devoted to the preservation of the *status quo*. White, conservative populists coalesced with other conservative elements into a nationalist movement dedicated to acquiring social and political power as the instruments of returning the United States to the *status quo ante*. At the grass-roots level, this conservative movement led to the emergence of an authoritarian populism which facilitated the rise of racially motivated violence. And at the national level, it provided the impetus for a coalition which elected Ronald Reagan to the presidency. One characterizes this movement as "white" in the literal sense that there was a marked absence of substantial African American participation in its activities or support for its values. Moreover, African American progress itself has become one of the primary targets of this movement in the attempt by the Reagan administration to rearticulate the racial problem in society in a way which subordinates African American and minority interests and restores and preserves white supremacy. (143–44)

After Reagan initiated and developed institutionalized racism and sexism while riding an ideological wave of white (and male and affluent) nationalism, Reagan's vice president, George H. W. Bush, ran for the presidency and won on the promise of more of the same.

If multiculturalism had experienced a slow demise before the turn of the new millennium, fading with institutional co-optation into a benign status, the events of September 11, 2001, would rush it to its grave, reigniting nationalist fervor in the United States. According to Bryson, the "post-9/11 theory" of culture became "If we don't defend our traditional American culture, we'll be obliterated by terrorists" (31). For the United States government and for many United States citizens who were old enough to understand the events that unfolded that day, the immediate response to the terrorist attacks of 9/11 was grounded in nationalism, and United States nationalism intensified in the years that followed the attacks. According to Paul T. McCartney, "enduring nationalist themes provided the basic structure in which Americans organized their comprehension of the reaction to the terrorist attacks," and, more specifically, George W. Bush employed "the legitimating power of nationalism to furnish the 'official' interpretation of September 11" (400). But the most vital transformation in United States nationalism after 9/11 came in its shift from a leadership role to a missionary role, and this missionary function of American nationalism was in effect the last nail in the coffin of multiculturalism.

Bush's response to 9/11 shifted nationalist policies from the traditional role of leading the rest of the world by example to changing the world "to suit American interests by making it more consistent with American values" (McCartney 400). McCartney explains that Bush's foreign policy following 9/11 was grounded in the strategic attempt to "change the world to make it look and act more like the United States," an extreme form of missionary nationalism that McCartney calls "vindicationism" (401). Nationalist vindicationism in the United States justifies the spread of American values (even by military force) because these values *should* be shared by all civilized nations. Nationalist vindicationism in the United States is based on American exceptionalism, or "the conviction that the United States is qualitatively different from—and better than—other states" (403). This exceptionalism has at times served the United States well, and English studies, after 9/11, reconnected with its old nationalist context, riding the wave of vindicationism. However, McCartney writes, "while American national identity has proven to be remarkably durable, current events suggest that it has become in some ways dangerously obsolete" (420). Thus, "it is time that Americans shed their self-identity as an exceptional people and accept instead their mature identity as integrated global citizens" (421). Although McCartney does not use this language, he would certainly agree that nationalism, in all of its varieties, has become a petrified and zombified discourse.

Interestingly, even before 9/11, sociolinguistics was the only discipline within English studies that was both founded on ideologies that value difference and also worked actively against nationalist ideologies. Sociolinguistics emerged during the late twentieth century as a direct challenge to the universality and nationalism assumed in structural linguistics, and, Hymes points out, "sociolinguistics in the modern world is inseparable from encounter with social change" (645). According to Linn, "Sociolinguistic analysis soon demonstrated that the standard languages" described by structural linguistics "were not cultural monoliths, there in perpetuity, but rather were the result of *processes* carried out by people intervening in the natural development of languages, of standardization, and, more than that, the standard languages served to perpetuate traditional and often outmoded social structures" (360). If structural linguistics served an American grand narrative of progress toward modernization (a narrative that legitimated white, male, affluent values by means of linguistic regulation), then sociolinguistics reversed this narrative. Linn explains that "in practice there is an increasing move towards the acceptability of language variation in a process, driven from below, of *destandardization*, of the debasement of the capital of standard languages" (373). Hymes agrees, explaining,

> Within the social matrix in which it acquires a system of grammar, a child acquires also a system of its use, regarding persons, places, purposes, other modes of communication, etc.—all the components of communicative events, together with attitudes and beliefs regarding them. There also develop patterns of the sequential use of language in conversation, address, standard routines, and the like. In such acquisition resides the child's *socio*linguistic competence (or, more broadly, communicative competence), its ability to participate in its society as not only a speaking, but also a communicating member. What children so acquire, an integrated theory of sociolinguistic description must be able to describe. (640)

If language is a process of destabilization (as Lynn argues), not a stable structure, and if language is acquired through its use in social contexts (as Hymes argues), not through standardized grammatical rules, then structural linguistics is merely the idealized invention of an imagined language with no connection to lived experience, diverse society, or practical communication.

Since sociolinguistics emphasizes the destabilization of language systems and contexts of language use, it serves the interests of globalization, cosmopolitanism, and planetarity very well.

## A New Context

Nationalism cannot drive ethical communication and action in a global, cosmopolitan, planetary society. Thus, McCartney holds out hope for a significant shift in the way Americans understand themselves in relation to the rest of the world, turning away from nationalism and toward cosmopolitanism: "if the broad contours of American national identity cannot be expected easily to change, then its more cosmopolitan elements should receive renewed emphasis in a manner better suited to the country's global stature" (401–2). Throughout the opening decades of the twenty-first century, the ideological gap between nationalist exceptionalism and cultural integrationism has been widening in the context of rapidly evolving communication and travel technologies that bare social differences and make cultural contact inevitable. The central problem with continuing to ground English studies in nationalism is that nationalist discourses have recently (or again) taken a nasty turn. Exclusionary nationalism fosters fear leading to distrust, hatred leading to violence, xenophobia leading to isolationism, and extremism leading to a small but highly motivated core of voting citizens.

English studies, in order to remain relevant in the twenty-first century and retain credibility in the modern university, must abandon its nationalist commitments and instead embrace globalization, cosmopolitanism, and planetarity as guiding concepts. In *Power in the Global Age*, Beck argues that globalization has replaced nationalism as the dominant discourse for explaining human life and social relations, and he offers cosmopolitanism as the way to surpass the dead (petrified, zombified) discourses of nationalism, objective science, and late capitalism. Beck writes,

> There are a number of signs pointing to the fact that a culture of globality is advancing upon us and possibly even gaining in dominance—among other things, the fact that, in the maelstrom

> of globalized modernization, global problems have long since become an everyday reality. Climate change, environmental destruction, food risks, global finance risks, migration, the anticipated consequences of innovations in genetics, human genetics, nanotechnology, and so forth, all serve to call into question in a quite tangible way the very foundations of social life. . . . In this one radically divided world, it is likely that security will only be achieved once people's willingness and ability to see the world of unrestrained modernity through the eyes of the other, through the lens of difference, have been awakened at a cultural level, and have become a part of our everyday existence. The task of creating a *cosmopolitan common sense* of this sort—a spirit of recognition of the difference of others which pervades ethnic, national, and religious traditions and brings them to life in the course of mutual exchange—is, after 11 September, no longer merely an idle, naïve verbal conjuring trick, but has become much more a question of survival. (xii–xiii)

If practitioners of English studies can move beyond the petrified and zombified discourse of nationalism, then they can also lead all other university subjects in the analysis, critique, and production of values and systems that drive modern globalization. Beck argues that the discourse of nationalism (especially "neo-nationalism") must be "countered intellectually, morally, and politically"; however, this "requires a change of perspective from the national to the cosmopolitan vision" (xiii). English studies should be a central disciplinary location within which this change is accomplished.

The issues related to globalization are not the province of specialized intellectual elites or powerful political operatives. Beck makes it clear that "*our daily lives* are profoundly influenced by the export of jobs, flexible production siting, information flows, global symbolic systems, and supranational organizations such as the World Bank, the International Monetary Fund, and the European Union" (xiv; emphasis added). If this is true, and I believe it is, then many accountants, lawyers, merchants, academics, and politicians (*especially* politicians), and so forth suffer from specialization sickness, a debilitatingly limited worldview. Beck argues that we are currently experiencing the destruction of nationalism as the predominant legitimating social force, and we are seeing its replacement with a cosmopolitan worldview, which does not entail "a clash of civilizations" but "the struggle for a human culture in which very different traditions are able to live alongside one another. . . . The new dangers facing humanity from the modern risk society make no distinctions of race, nation, or continent" (xv). English education scholar Gunther Kress agrees, saying, "I cannot imagine that the trends toward pluriculturalism will be reversed; I believe that they will intensify. The simple facts of globalization, and of the technologies of transport, make it inevitable. The gradual disintegration of nation-states which we are witnessing at the moment will continue, and, I think, accelerate" (*Writing* 13). This rapidly emerging global world, Kress writes, "will have to be one in which difference is seen as a resource for productive lives and for innovative encounters with problems" (*Writing* 13).

More specifically, according to Beck, cosmopolitanism seeks and embraces "the values of an acknowledged, lived diversity that pervade every social institution and historical context, a 'cosmopolitan common sense' that takes hold of large sections of humanity and enables them to shape seemingly unstoppable developments" (xv). Cosmopolitanism, then, is Beck's answer to the demise of petrified and zombified discourses like nationalism, and, he writes, "it *might just* make the improbable possible, namely the survival of humanity beyond the twenty-first century without a lapse back into barbarism" (xvi). If Beck is right that modern society is in "the twilight zone between the passing of the national era and the emergence of the cosmopolitan era" (2), then now is the time for English studies to reframe its contents, ideologies, and methods to align with this emerging worldview or risk petrification, zombification, or, worse, irrelevance. Beck asserts that "the national outlook is *wrong* . . . [and] only the cosmopolitan outlook *adequately fits with reality* and provides an *adequate basis for action*. . . . Those who remain caught up within the national outlook will find they have lost out" (110).

Although Beck considers globalization to be a general condition of human existence and cosmopolitanism to be a social practice within a global context, these two terms (*globalization* and *cosmopolitanism*) actually have contested meanings. For some theorists, globalization refers specifically to the imposition of Western economic systems on societies that do not necessarily desire or benefit from those systems. For others, like Beck, it refers more generally to the recent advances in travel and communication technologies that make contact among cultures unavoidable. For some theorists, cosmopolitanism refers specifically to the orientalist interest in other cultures as a source of fascination and a form of entertainment. For others, like Beck, it refers more generally to a dialectical recognition of social equality, an appreciation of cultural difference, and an expansion of global understanding. With Beck, I understand these two terms (*globalization* and *cosmopolitanism*) in their more general senses.

Nevertheless, a third term has emerged recently that negotiates these competing senses of globalization and cosmopolitanism—*planetarity*. In *Death of a Discipline*, Gayatri Chakravorty Spivak explains that planetarity refers to "an undifferentiated 'natural' space rather than a differentiated political space" (72), and she offers planetarity as a remedy for the petrified and zombified discourses of comparative literature. According to Spivak, although comparative literature does value difference, it does so within an anti-nationalist framework, which, despite its *anti-* prefix, remains within the general scope of nationalist discourses. Thus, comparative literature must push its sense of difference outside the ideological boundaries of anti-nationalism and place it, instead, within planetarity. What planetarity offers is a framework in which alterity is the starting point: "The planet is in the species of alterity, belonging to another system; and yet we inhabit it, on loan" (72). Since the planet (not humanity) is the center of all beliefs and activities, and the planet is a source of difference, not a center of ideological gravity, human practical lives and cultural homes become inherently "uncanny" (74). Planetarity implies, according to Spivak, "the defamiliarization of familiar space" (77), a "project of other-ing the subject" (82).

After Spivak reframed difference and alterity as the center of human activity through the trope of planetarity, other scholars shifted the meaning of planetarity more toward material (rather than figurative) referents. For example, Amy J. Elias and Christian Moraru describe planetarity in material ways, invoking ecological crisis as the exigence for aesthetic production (and, I would add, the analysis, critique, and production of discourse in social context). According to Elias and Moraru, planetarity is relational and ethical. Elias and Moraru write,

> [I]f today's planetary life consists in an incessantly thickening, historically unprecedented web of relations among people, cultures, and locales, to comprehend the planetary must entail grasping the relationality embedded in it. Consequently, relatedness, dialogue, and interactivity are central to major aesthetic initiatives stirring at this stage in world history. (xii)

Further, like cosmopolitanism, planetarity extends beyond pure relationality and into "the vital problem of *ethical relation*," which precludes the colonizing impulse to impose hegemonic structures (economic, cultural) on others. While globalization and cosmopolitanism may imply specific kinds of relationality among humans and their cultures, "the twenty-first century is witnessing the rise of a broader, postnational formation, which is the planet" (xxv).

Dividing English studies curricula by nation and period presents obstacles to the advancement of the discipline in a global, cosmopolitan, planetary society because the structures of nation and period cannot evolve in response to discursive contexts that are shifting the balance of cultural and academic values toward difference. Clausen agrees, writing,

> The concept of "national literatures" in English has outlived its usefulness and should be abandoned, both as a way of thinking about literary history and as a way of organizing curricula. . . . [T]he nationalisms that gave rise successively to the concept of a distinctly British literature, then an American literature, and now Australian, Canadian, and a host of what are often described equivocally as "new literatures," constitute a barrier to clear thinking about what has long since become an international enterprise carried on in many cultural settings. . . . (61)

And, Clausen continues, "the convention of dividing [literature] along national lines exaggerates a particular kind of difference, does violence to the ways in which literary influence works, and serves purposes that need to be scrutinized rather than accepted without reflection as obvious or worthy" (62–63). The fact is, Clausen explains, "literary curricula were delineated according to nationalistic assumptions that, when examined today, look philosophically dubious and thoroughly old-fashioned" (64). In order for English studies to remain current and relevant in a new context that emphasizes global culture and cosmopolitan attitudes, this aging discipline will need to embrace the idea that *curriculum matters*.

## Curriculum Matters

Curricula are not lists of assignments, books, and courses; they are structures of cultural values that are represented by and propagated through lists of assignments, books, and courses, intentionally selected and purposefully constructed in order to condition students to become certain kinds of citizens. When we lose sight of the values inherent in the materials and methods that make up our curricula, we lose sight of the very reason that curriculum matters. Kress agrees:

> A curriculum is a design for a future social subject, and via that envisioned subject a design for a future society. That is, the curriculum puts forward knowledges, skills, meanings, and values in the present which will be telling in the lives of those who experience the curriculum ten or twenty years later. Forms of pedagogy experienced by children now in school suggest to them forms of social relations which they are encouraged to adopt, adapt, modify, and treat as models. The curriculum, and its associated pedagogy, puts forward a set of cultural, linguistic, and social resources in relation to which (among others) students constantly construct, reconstruct, and transform their subjectivity. Such a view of the curriculum and of pedagogy requires that those who construct the curriculum have a vision of the future in which this subject, here and now experiencing the curriculum, will lead her or his life—a culturally, personally, socially productive life, one hopes. ("Representational" 16)

To prepare students for life in a global, cosmopolitan, and planetary world, English studies must look toward the future, not the past, to find its inspiration for reform.

English studies should commit its future to designing and implementing new curricular models that (1) embody cultural values consistent with our emerging global, cosmopolitan, and planetary society; (2) cultivate global, cosmopolitan, and planetary attitudes toward difference and identification; and (3) facilitate adaptive practices in constantly evolving contexts. Kress writes, "Where my message is new is in its attempts to think of curriculum overtly and directly in relation to likely social, economic, and political changes, in relation to likely futures, and in its thinking of the English curriculum as a central means of *intervention*, as a crucial factor in participating in the construction of those futures" (*Writing* 15). The new English "curriculum should envisage, project, and aim to produce an individual who is at ease with difference and change, whose fundamental being values innovation and is therefore able to question, to challenge, and above all to *propose alternatives, constructively*" (*Writing* 29).

But shifting English curriculum from a conservative structure founded on tradition to a progressive process founded on adaptive practices will not be easy. For most English departments today, a change like this would be radical. Such a change is predicated on moving English studies curriculum away from its current "content orientation," as Hayles puts it, and toward a "problem orientation" (9). According to Hayles, in order to remain relevant in the twenty-first century, English studies must break the bonds of critical writing and make a move toward problem-based production. However, this move requires more than just a new set of books for teaching; it requires a complete shift in content and ideology. The shift in content requires the recognition that all of the disciplines that make up English studies have an equal role to play in establishing legitimate objects of study, and the shift in ideology requires the easing of the aesthetic privilege in English studies and a recognition that in a global society, survival requires, too, a pragmatic ideology.

There have been countless laments that English studies is in crisis. However, as James F. English explains, global English studies is thriving. English writes, "despite all the challenges facing students and educators today, our discipline has not reached a precipice of especial vulnerability. If we step back from our local positions and consider the global future of English studies, there is little to suggest it is fading away" (8). An English studies that recognizes and embraces its global, cosmopolitan, and planetary future will thrive, but this recognition is obscured by traditional disciplinary structures that do not support global engagement. It is not enough just to critique nationalism and periodization. In order to succeed, English studies will have to produce new discursive structures and processes within which to conduct its work, and all of the disciplines that make up English studies (linguistics, rhetoric and composition, creative writing, literature and literary criticism, critical theory and cultural studies, and English education) must be understood as equal participants in this disciplinary effort.

To this end, I propose seven principles to guide English studies' evolution toward increasing relevance in the twenty-first century: (1) conceive the discipline as a process; (2) seek difference; (3) expand what counts as literature; (4) promote adaptive practices; (5) value technology; (6) embrace collaboration; and (7) take a public turn.

*Conceive the discipline as a process.* Academic disciplines emerge and develop through the interaction of many intersecting forces: social context, cultural relevance, government financing, university missions, means of professionalization, collective purpose, methods of inquiry, curriculum, pedagogy, subject matter, and practical application. Since each one of these forces is in constant flux, and since the interactions among fluid forces are often unpredictable, the nature of disciplinarity is (or should be) more an integrative process than a static structure. David R. Shumway and Ellen Messer-Davidow explain that "knowledge is historically and socially contingent" (218), which requires disciplines and their practitioners to adapt to shifting epistemological constraints and to evolve in relation to historical circumstances. Robert Post agrees, arguing that

> [a]lthough the institutionalization of disciplines and the intersubjective character of disciplinary norms make disciplines resistant to alteration, disciplines nevertheless grow and evolve. The practices of disciplines are continuously adjusting to the changing interests of disciplinary practitioners and to the emergent demands placed on disciplines by exogenous forces like universities and society at large. Disciplines also evolve in response to the unfolding of their own internal logic. They

> sometimes splinter and sometimes merge. Disciplines can be born and they can die. (753)

Disciplines that do not evolve are generally the ones that die.

Students, teachers, writers, scholars, and administrators who view their disciplines as processes constantly invent new methods and incorporate new subject matters into their activities, adapting their work to the flux of forces that constitute and influence disciplinarity. In the context of higher education, where disciplines are always coming and going, adaptability means survival. The humanities in general and English studies in particular are facing an increasingly global, cosmopolitan, and planetary context in which cultures interact and difference predominates. Conceiving English studies as a process means understanding the disciplines that make up English departments not as separate categories of unrelated work but as a networked assemblage of functions that interrelate and support each other in powerful ways.

*Seek difference.* Difference is epistemic. The conservative preservation of identity-structures (like nationalism) leads to intellectual stagnation, whereas the progressive pursuit of difference expands understanding and generates new knowledge. Commenting on the disintegration of nationalist discourses into political chaos during the 1980s, Jacques Derrida argues that unified notions of culture are no longer viable. Derrida explains that culture must evolve from a unified structure to "a culture of oneself *as* a culture *of* the other . . . of the *difference to oneself*" (10). Seeking difference as a source of dynamic (not petrified or zombified) knowledge is integral to Spivak's desire for "making home uncanny" (76), which is a central principle of planetarity. It is the "defamiliarization of familiar space" (77), understanding difference as a generative force.

Seeking difference must move beyond the pursuit of cultural entertainment and exotic curiosity, which leaves a unified culture intact, unaffected (or even reinforced) by the strangeness of the Other. In *Anthropology as Cultural Critique*, George E. Marcus and Michael M. J. Fischer offer critical ethnography as a methodology for making difference epistemic. Critical ethnography entails "defamiliarization by cross-cultural juxtaposition" (138), or the dialectical critique of two or more cultures simultaneously, including one's own. According to Marcus and Fischer, "this technique entails using detailed ethnography of cultures abroad, with special care not to remove them from their contemporary situations, as a critical and comparative probe for some equally intensive project of ethnography *at home*" (157; emphasis added). Traditional ethnography presumes the cultural objectivity of the scientific observer's description of the Other. However, critical ethnography understands all cultures to be equal, with difference as the generating principle for *self*-knowledge. In order for English studies to adapt to the changing contexts of globalization, cosmopolitanism, and planetarity, it will have to embrace critical ethnography as a new method for designing courses and curricula.

*Expand what counts as literature.* To accomplish the goals of abandoning nationalist discourses and integrating the disciplines of English studies into a powerful assemblage that values difference and promotes understanding, the practitioners of English studies (students, teachers, writers, scholars, and administrators) will have to expand their notions of what counts as literature. In this renewed concept of English studies, literature shifts from texts valued according to white, male, affluent criteria (the canon) to all culturally salient texts, regardless of the race, gender, or class of their authors. In *Literary Theory: An Introduction*, Terry Eagleton agrees, writing, "There is no 'essence' of literature whatsoever. Any bit of writing may be read 'non-pragmatically,' if that is what reading a text as literature means, just as any writing may be read 'poetically. . . .' Perhaps 'literature' means . . . any kind of writing which for some reason or another somebody values highly" (8). Thus, Eagleton concludes, "Any belief that the study of literature is the study of a stable, well-definable entity, as entomology is the study of insects, can be abandoned as a chimera" (9). Not all cultures produce written texts that fit neatly into the aesthetics of the traditional literary canon, so what counts as "literature" must expand if English studies is to remain relevant in the context of a global world.

At the same time that we expand what counts as literature, we also need to expand what counts as a text. Texts are not just words on pages; they are any semiotic mode on or in any medium. Material objects and visual images, all of which communicate semiotically as effectively as do words on the page, should count as texts in a reformulated English studies for a global, cosmopolitan, and planetary context. In a global, cosmopolitan, and planetary world, multimodal (material, visual, aural, and verbal) communication may become more efficient and effective than verbal communication alone. Kress writes,

> The new English curriculum will need to recognize these new forms of texts, with all their vast consequences, in their effects on the humans who make and use them. The currently dominant mode in relation to these changes is one of pessimism. Trained as we are, formed as subjects as we are in a culture in which the written word was central, the move to the visual fills us with nostalgia and foreboding. That, however, is *our* problem: it is not the problem of the new generation unless we make it so, unless we make it our business to make them live their futures in the image of our pasts. (*Writing* 28)

In fact, Kress continues, "The visual and the multimodal may represent the essential means of information management in the coming period. The English curriculum will need a stance on that" (*Writing* 29).

*Promote adaptive practices.* Globalization, cosmopolitanism, and planetarity imply an engagement of cultures that emphasizes the uncanny, the unfamiliar. Processes of innovation and adaptive practices are necessary to ensure ethical engagement. Kress suggests that the central role of the English curriculum in the context of globalization is to instill in its students the "ability to see change and difference as entirely usual conditions of cultural and social life; *and* to see them as essential productive resources" (*Writing* 3). This transition from change and difference as conditions of life to productive resources requires a curricular shift from critique to adaptive practices. Thus, for Kress, the survival of English as an academic subject requires its practitioners to "move beyond critique as an aim in itself, to the proposal of alternatives as a new and necessary aim" (*Writing* 4). Yet proposing alternatives is not possible in the context of a disciplinary discourse dominated by aesthetic criticism, which often devalues production as unimportant.

Adaptive practices require both a conceptual understanding of the representational resources (or affordances) offered by each technology (print or digital) and also the practical experience of judging which resources are most useful for solving real problems. Hayles offers comparative media studies as a form of "problem-based inquiry" within which to accomplish these conceptual and practical goals. Hayles writes,

> Comparative Media Studies can provide a framework for courses in which students would acquire a wide repertoire of strategies to address complex problems. Faced with a particular kind of problem, they would not be confined to only one mode of address but could think creatively about the resources, approaches, and strategies the problem requires and choose the more promising one, or an appropriate combination of two or more, for a given context. (8–9)[4]

"Comparative Media Studies," Hayles writes, "is well suited to this role and can approach it through the framework of multiple literacies," joining "theory and practice through the productive work of making" (9).[5] While analysis and critique remain important in any conception of English studies, without production, all knowledge generated in and through the discipline will die with it.

*Value technology.* Technologies and humans evolve together, making technology a necessary and central subject for humanistic study. Understanding technologies as nothing more than material objects ignores their social and practical uses; understanding human communication as nothing more than the translation of thought into symbols ignores its symbiotic relationship with technologies. In *How We Think*, Hayles calls the coevolution of technologies and humans "technogenesis" (10), and she argues that it is time for humanities scholars to recognize and investigate the technogenetic interdependency of human thought and the technologies that condition its production and enable its distribution.

Multimodal communication is enabled by technology. If it is a goal of English studies to foster confidence in the face of cultural change and construct alternatives to waning social ideologies and discourses, and if technology both reflects and drives these cultural and social changes, then English studies cannot afford to ignore the influence of technology on the discipline. Since English studies is the analysis, critique, and production of discourse in social context, then English studies will have to come to grips with the technologies through which discourses are produced, distributed, and consumed. Although in English studies, words have long held hegemonic power over all other modes of representation, it is time to reject this constraint and understand English studies as a process (analysis, critique, and production) that can function in any medium at all, including words, but also including images, sounds, and objects.

*Embrace collaboration.* Planetarity leads practitioners of English studies in the direction of integrative (dialogic, interactive) work. Adaptive practices are inherently integrative in attitude, and when practitioners of a discipline are educated into specialized limitations, collaboration increases the possibility for innovative work that recognizes evolving contexts. Collaboration requires a move toward identification without threat to identity. Unlike the history of African American, Asian American, Latin American, and Native American writers, whose very identities were threatened by identification with a white culture that framed them as Other, collaboration retains identity as a resource in the process of identification. In other words, identification is a drive toward integration that maintains the integrity of identity and uses difference as a resource to produce something new. If we begin our work from a place of planetary alterity (rather than a place of national identity), we can approach collaboration in new ways, as a means to defamiliarize our own orientation to English studies and expand what it means to practice the discipline.

*Take a public turn.* Globalization, cosmopolitanism, and planetarity are not categories of academic specialization; they are descriptions of lived experience, and, as such, they exercise powerful influence over every public institution, including higher education. And globalization, cosmopolitanism, and planetarity do not describe theoretical positions but everyday life, and they do not choose whom to affect (gender, class, race, sexuality), since they affect all of us equally. Thus, it is the ethical responsibility of English studies to address these issues not only in classrooms, journals, and university presses, but also in blogs, newspapers, and magazines. The central problem with taking the public turn is that publications in these public venues are not valued by universities or English departments, and thus they do not count toward merit raises, tenure, or promotion. This is the insularity of academic English that will lead to its own demise. In order to respond to the shifting discourses outside of academic boundaries and in order to signal that response, English studies will also have to shift its institutional reward systems from "publication" to "*public*-ation."

## Conclusion

Each chapter in this book examines a different discipline within English studies from the perspective of *difference*. Jacquelyn Rahman explores linguistics as a way to understand and value different cultural dialects, emphasizing the generative possibilities of sociolinguistics. Victor Villanueva emphasizes contrastive rhetorics and the positive effects they have had on composition studies' perspective of difference in writing. Sarah Sandman discusses the place of LGBTQ+ identities in the discourse of creative writing, both academic and public. Richard C. Taylor proposes a new focus on transnational literatures as a means to understand ourselves and others in new and productive ways. Jeffrey J. Williams examines how cultural studies and critical theory expand the work of criticism in order to form a new global humanities. And Tonya B. Perry promotes urban education as a site where difference is epistemic, and teachers must emphasize adaptive pedagogical practices in addition to acquiring and conveying content knowledge. Each chapter, in its own way, proposes new frameworks for understanding English studies as a response to the discourses of globalization, cosmopolitanism, and planetarity that are forming new contexts for academic work. This book, then, is not just a description of English studies—it is also an argument for *the difference it makes.*

## Notes

1. The Morrill Act of 1862 stipulates that at least 30,000 acres of public (nonmineral) land should be allocated to each state for every Congressional representative it has, with at least one college constructed and opened within five years of the allocation. Interestingly, this act limits the offer of state land for the construction of universities only to the twenty-three existing Union states: "No State while in a condition of rebellion or insurrection against the government of the United States shall be entitled to the benefit of this act." Since the eleven Confederate states were in rebellion and insurrection against the Northern government, they were denied funds provided by the first Morrill Act (not that they would have accepted them anyway). Here we see education as a significant weapon used in a war against slavery and racial injustice. Southern slave owners denied education to slaves in order to establish and maintain their subjection. Northern politicians denied funds for universities to Confederate, slave-owning states in order to establish and maintain their subjection, their inability to train a workforce able to respond to infrastructural crises that debilitated both rural and urban life in the South.

Following the Civil War, it would take until 1890 for Congress to pass a second Morrill Act, again emphasizing science, discovery, and specialization, and allotting cash (not public land) for Southern states to establish legally recognized "land grant" colleges, as long as those Southern states could prove that their admission standards were not based on race, or they established separate colleges for freed slaves (what would become HBCUs). These land grant universities were tuition-free, supplemented by the states that established them, and open to all citizens willing to learn a trade that would relieve the country's infrastructural crises.

2. Following the assassination of the Austrian Archduke Franz Ferdinand in 1914, a far-flung military conflict emerged with Russia, France, Italy, Japan, and Great Britain as allies aligned against Germany, Austria-Hungary, and Turkey. The United States would not join forces with the allies until 1917, but United States troops would be instrumental in overwhelming the German military and forcing their leaders to sign an armistice agreement in 1918.

3. In the decades preceding World War I, the economic foundation of the far-flung British Empire had begun to weaken due to competition from capitalist upstart nations like the United States and Germany. Terry Eagleton writes, "The era of the academic establishment of English is also the era of high imperialism in England. As British capitalism became threatened and progressively outstripped by its younger German and American rivals, the squalid, undignified scramble of too much capital chasing too few overseas territories, which was to culminate in 1914 in the first imperialist world war, created the urgent need for a sense of national mission and identity. What was at stake in English studies was less English *literature* than *English* literature: our great 'national poets' Shakespeare and Milton, the sense of an 'organic' national tradition and identity to which new recruits could be admitted by the study of humane letters" (24). Eagleton continues, "One of the most strenuous antagonists of English—philology—was closely bound up with Germanic influence; and since England happened to be passing through a major war with Germany, it was possible to smear classical philology as a form of ponderous Teutonic nonsense with which no self-respecting Englishman should be caught associating. England's victory over Germany meant a renewal of national pride, an upsurge of patriotism which could only aid English's cause" (25–26). Thus, in Great Britain, Eagleton explains, "English Literature rode to power on the back of wartime nationalism" (26), and English achieved its power rapidly: "In the early 1920s it was desperately unclear why English was worth studying at all; by the early 1930s it had become a question of why it was worth wasting your time on anything else" (27).

4. Hayles explains, "Such a curriculum [comparative media studies] is worlds away from the offerings of a traditional English department, which typically focuses on periodizations (e.g., eighteenth century prose), nationalities (British, American, Anglophone, etc.), and genres (fiction, prose, drama). The difficulties with this kind of approach are not only that it is outmoded and fails to account for what much of contemporary scholarship is about (postcolonial studies, globalization studies, race and gender studies, etc.). It also focuses on content rather than problems, assuming that students will somehow make the leap from classroom exercises to real world complexities by themselves" (9).

5. I am struck by how similar Hayles's definition of comparative media studies is to Aristotle's definition of a *techne* (or art). Aristotle explains that a *techne* is a "reasoned habit of mind in making" (*Nichomachean Ethics*, 6.4; qtd in Kennedy 289). Hayles is thus turning the word *technology* away from its current material sense and back toward its etymological origin as a theoretical and practical means of *production*.

## Works Cited

Beck, Ulrich. *Power in the Global Age*. Translated by Kathleen Cross, Polity Press, 2005.

Brass, Jory. "Constituting a Sense of 'American' Identity and Place through Language and Literary Study: A Curriculum History, 1898–1912." *English Teaching: Practice and Critique*, vol. 12, no. 2, Sept. 2013, pp. 41–57. http://education.waikato.ac.nz/research/files/etpc/files/2013v12n2art3.pdf.

Bryson, Bethany. *Making Multiculturalism: Boundaries and Meaning in U.S. English Departments*. Stanford UP, 2005.

Butcher, Philip. "Creative Writing in the Negro College." *The Journal of Negro Education*, vol. 20, no. 2, spring 1951, pp. 160–63. *JSTOR*, www.jstor.org/stable/2966461.

Chon-Smith, Chong. "The Asian American Writing Movement and Black Radicalism: Race and Gender Politics in Multiethnic Anthologies." *Journal of Black Studies*, vol. 45, no. 8, Nov. 2014, pp. 708–30. *JSTOR*, www.jstor.org/stable/24573590.

Clausen, Christopher. "'National Literatures' in English: Toward a New Paradigm." *New Literary History*, vol. 25, no. 1, winter 1994, pp. 61–72. *JSTOR*, www.jstor.org/stable/469440.

Eagleton, Terry. *Literary Theory: An Introduction*. 2nd ed., U of Minnesota P, 1996.

Elias, Amy J., and Christian Moraru. "Introduction: The Planetary Condition." *The Planetary Turn: Relationality and Geoaesthetics in the Twenty-First Century*, edited by Amy J. Elias and Christian Moraru, Northwestern UP, 2015, pp. xi–xxxvii.

English, James F. *The Global Future of English Studies*. Wiley-Blackwell, 2012.

Gere, Anne Ruggles. "The Teaching of Writing: 1912–2010." *Reading the Past, Writing the Future: A Century of American Literacy Education and the National Council of Teachers of English*, edited by Erika Lindemann, National Council of Teachers of English, 2010, pp. 93–121.

Giroux, Henry A. "White Nationalism, Armed Culture, and State Violence in the Age of Donald Trump." *Philosophy and Social Criticism*, vol. 43, no. 9, 2017, pp. 887–910, doi: 10.1177/0191453717702800.

Hayles, N. Katherine. *How We Think: Digital Media and Contemporary Technogenesis*. Chicago UP, 2012.

Hymes, Dell. "Why Linguistics Needs the Sociologist." *Social Research*, vol. 34, no. 4, winter 1967, pp. 632–47. *JSTOR*, www.jstor.org/stable/40970747.

Kennedy, George A. *Aristotle on Rhetoric: A Theory of Civic Discourse*. Oxford UP, 1991.

King, James C. "Nationalism." *American Journal of Sociology*, vol. 39, no. 6, May 1934, pp. 818–26. *JSTOR*, www.jstor.org/stable/2767427.

Kramer, Lloyd. "Historical Narratives and the Meaning of Nationalism." *Journal of the History of Ideas*, vol. 58, no. 3, July 1997, pp. 525–45. *JSTOR*, www.jstor.org/stable/3653913.

Kress, Gunther. "Representational Resources and the Production of Subjectivity: Questions for the Theoretical Development of Critical Discourse Analysis in a Multicultural Society." *Texts and Practices: Readings in Critical Discourse Analysis*, edited by Carmen Rosa Caldas-Coulthard and Malcolm Coulthard. Routledge, 1996, pp. 15–31.

———. *Writing the Future: English and the Making of a Culture of Innovation*. NCTE, 1995.

Linn, Andrew. "Vernaculars and the Idea of a Standardized Language." *The Oxford Handbook of the History of Linguistics*, edited by Keith Allan, Oxford UP, 2013, pp. 359–74.

Lowrie, S. Gale. "Nationalism." *International Journal of Ethics*, vol. 41, no. 1, Oct. 1930, pp. 35–49. *JSTOR*, www.jstor.org/stable/2377943.

Marcus, George E., and Michael M. J. Fischer. *Anthropology as Cultural Critique: An Experimental Moment in Human Sciences*, University of Chicago Press, 1986.

Marcuse, Herbert. *One Dimensional Man*. Beacon Press, 1964.

McCartney, Paul T. "American Nationalism and U.S. Foreign Policy from September 11 to the Iraq War." *Political Science Quarterly*, vol. 119, no. 3, 2004, pp. 399–423. *JSTOR*, www.jstor.org/stable/20202389.

Morrill Act (1862), www.ourdocuments.gov/doc.php?flash=false&doc=33.

Myers, D. G. *The Elephants Teach: Creative Writing Since 1880.* University of Chicago Press, 2006.

Post, Robert. "Debating Disciplinarity." *Critical Inquiry*, vol. 35, no. 4, summer 2009, pp. 749–70. *JSTOR*, www.jstor.org/stable/10.1086/599580.

Redding, Saunders. "The Problems of the Negro Writer." *The Massachusetts Review*, vol. 6, no. 1, autumn 1964–1965, pp. 57–70. *JSTOR*, www.jstor.org/stable/25087221.

Renker, Elizabeth. "Resistance and Change: The Rise of American Literature Studies." *American Literature*, vol. 64, no. 2, June 1992, pp. 347–65. *JSTOR*, www.jstor.org/stable/2927840.

Shumway, David R., and Ellen Messer-Davidow. "Disciplinarity: An Introduction." *Poetics Today*, vol. 12, no. 2, summer 1991, pp. 201–25. *JSTOR*, www.jstor.org/stable/1772850.

Spivak, Gayatri Chakravorty. *Death of a Discipline.* Columbia UP, 2003.

Walters, Ronald. "White Racial Nationalism in the United States." *Urban League Review*, vol. 13, nos. 1–2, summer–winter 1989, pp. 141–64.

Washburn, Kathleen. "New Indians and Indigenous Archives." *PMLA*, vol. 127, No. 2, Mar. 2012, pp. 380–84. *JSTOR*, www.jstor.org/stable/41616831.

Wright, Richard. "Blueprint for Negro Writing." *Within the Circle: An Anthology of African American Literary Criticism from the Harlem Renaissance to the Present*, edited by Angelyn Mitchell, Duke UP, 1994, pp. 97–106.

Chapter One

# *Linguistics*

Jacquelyn Rahman
*Miami University*

## Background

At a time when understanding and appreciation of varied American cultures is critical, English departments are in a favored position to exert a positive influence in promoting acceptance of diversity. As a subfield of English studies, linguistics has the potential to offer unique contributions to the implementation of approaches that develop in students' open-mindedness and appreciation of difference, skills that will be to their advantage as they move into a rapidly changing world.

While most linguists work in independent linguistics departments, the Linguistic Society of America reports that a significant number are based in or are affiliated with English departments. There, their schedules often include courses in prescriptive grammar, history of English, and topics related to applied linguistics. Linguists are happy to teach these courses, but they are often only distantly related to those linguists' areas of expertise. Linguists are capable in a wide range of areas, but they may be underutilized as a resource for teaching, program development, and collaboration with other faculty in English studies programs.

Courses in various areas of English studies can enrich the experience of linguistics majors. By the same token, linguistics courses can be useful as part of the program for students focusing on areas such as literature and creative writing. Courses in linguistics offer new ways of understanding topics like metaphor, word formation, and sound symbolism. Sociolinguistics courses create an awareness of the nature and structure of regional, social, and ethnic dialects. They offer insight into individual differences in speech and various dimensions of language use in society.

Linguistics is able to attract students from across a university into a course in English studies. Many institutions require students to complete a course that enhances logic and formal reasoning; a survey course in linguistics is generally able to meet this requirement while providing engagement with the language of diverse social groups. This is true of courses in syntax, morphology, and phonology as well.

The field of linguistics contains eleven major subfields. Many linguistics faculty members can teach undergraduate courses in several of these areas. Here is a list of branches with brief descriptions. (Some linguists might merge or expand a few of the headings.)

*Syntax* analyzes ways in which words combine in a given language in order to produce sentences that speakers consider well formed.

*Morphology* studies the way words are formed from small units that have meaning or function.

*Phonology* analyzes the sound systems of languages and dialects, the vowels and consonants comprising the inventory, and the relationships among them.

*Phonetics* studies speech sounds and how people process and produce them.

*Semantics* studies the meanings of words and the ways in which words interact with syntax to create meaning.

*Psycholinguistics* studies the relationships among language, the mind, and the brain.

*Pragmatics* examines language in use with consideration of matters such as background assumptions, attitudes, and intentions of speakers and listeners.

*Historical linguistics* examines the development of language through time.

*Sociolinguistics* studies language in its social contexts through traditions such as ethnography, dialectology, and variation studies.

*Applied linguistics* examines language in practical activities, as in TESOL.

*Computational linguistics* simulates language processes.

All of the subfields of linguistics can contribute to the offerings of a forward-looking English department. They share interests with other branches of English studies, but they are characterized by distinctive features that complement and are complemented by other subjects. Linguistics straddles two domains in the academic world: while emphasis is on the humanistic study of language, linguists also employ scientific methods to accomplish their goals. In addition, most of the subfields listed above focus primarily on spoken language, while the norm in other subfields of English studies has traditionally been the creation and analysis of written texts.

This chapter explores some of the ways in which linguistics can be an integral component of an English studies program, adding a dimension to the intellectual life of both faculty and students. The greatest emphasis of the chapter is on sociolinguistics, the study of language in society. This subfield is particularly amenable to integration into a progressive program of English studies, since its mission inherently assumes acknowledgment of the naturalness of language diversity and a commitment to attempting to understand it.

Sociolinguistics is my primary field of research. Much of my work has an implied theme of social justice, often addressing issues related to the semiotic power of linguistic features to activate stereotypes and biases. For example, linguistic features of the ethnic variety spoken by some African Americans have long been regarded as debased English, the target of "Ebonics" jokes. Yet African American English (AAE), like all other languages and dialects, is governed by a precise system of linguistic rules. In another instance, Hispanics living in a largely homogenous community such as El Paso, Texas, may speak a variety of English consisting primarily of mainstream grammar and lexicon with Spanish features of pronunciation (Fought). Because of their ethnic speech patterns, these speakers may be seen as immigrants and learners of English, even if they were born and raised in the United States. They may not even have knowledge of Spanish (Fought).

A major subtext across contemporary linguistics is that all languages and dialects are equal in their systematicity and ability to convey information. While structural variation exists, communication adheres to certain universal principles. Rosina

Lippi-Green notes, "All spoken languages are equally capable of conveying a full range of ideas, experiences, and developing to meet new needs as they arise" (8). As this chapter shows, linguists did not always believe this. A realization of the universality of underlying principles and structural logic present among diverse languages is relatively new in the field.

A question is how linguistics came to a point where it can contribute to efforts to destroy notions of superiority in language. Sociolinguistics, like the other subfields, has evolved over time, under the influence of various contexts. All have developed under a system that favors white, educated classes and, in particular, males in that group. An assumption of whiteness as superior and normative has colored the work of scholars for centuries. Along with that, the language of whites has been considered ideal.

Carl Meinhof, an eminent linguist of the early twentieth century, expressed a common view when he made the following statement about the language of African Americans' African forebears: "We are dealing with the tongues of barbarians . . . which are supposed to consist of half-bestial sounds, not similar or comparable to any civilized language. There we have an elaborate grammatical structure, shaped through successive centuries . . . here, a primitive barbarian, necessarily devoid of every semblance of polish and refinement" (3–4).

I devote considerable time to discussing the ethnic language employed by some members of the African American community because it occupies a unique position among varieties of English. Walt Wolfram and Natalie Schilling describe AAE as the "paradigmatic case of ethnicity-based language diversity" (217). They observe that studies in AAE "eclipse those in other social and regional varieties of American English, with more than five times as many publications devoted to AAE than any other American dialect" (Wolfram and Schilling 217; also see Baugh, *Out of the Mouths of Slaves* and *Black Street Speech*; Patrick; Rickford; Rickford and Rickford; Rickford, Sweetland, Rickford, and Grano).

Understanding AAE and how it arose can play a role in diminishing stereotypes related to AAE and, by extension, to varieties spoken by other marginalized groups. African American English emerged from a confluence of speakers of diverse African languages, stolen from their homelands and thrown together under the harsh conditions of slavery. These captives were highly motivated to develop a code of communication for survival.

The adverse circumstances under which they were still able to create a coherent and multilayered variety of language also make AAE an ideal model for studying principles of linguistics. The language-making faculty that is universally present among humans allowed these captives to create a code that is systemic and rules governed. This chapter gives attention to several varieties, such as Chicano English, Appalachian English, and the language of natives of Martha's Vineyard in New England.

To better understand how linguistics matured and began trying to shed its biases, it is useful to review the work of scholars who laid the groundwork for the discipline. In many instances, steps taken in earlier stages of the field point to contemporary methods of study, while in other cases, old ways precipitated the development of revolutionary approaches.

## Brief History of Modern Linguistics

Ways of thinking that developed in eighteenth century Europe set the tone for attitudes that linguistics scholars are still attempting to dispel. In 1711 the Swiss botanist Carl Linnaeus published a hierarchy of what he saw as human evolution. He assigned colors to the "races," labeling Europeans *white*, Africans *black*, and other perceived groups as *red* and *yellow*. Whites stood at the top of the hierarchy. Linnaeus's hierarchy and other similar ones were linked to an ideology of white superiority that served to justify colonialism and the highly lucrative transatlantic slave trade (Kendi). It was in this climate that modern linguistics began (Rahman, *N Word Papers*).

Between 1907 and 1911, Ferdinand de Saussure, another Swiss scholar, delivered a series of lectures later published as *Course in General Linguistics*. Dissemination of Saussure's ideas reshaped many of the beliefs scholars had previously held about the study of language and marked the founding of the structuralist school of linguistics. Moving away from his philological background, Saussure argued that language exists as a system that allows speakers to produce comprehensible speech. He saw that rules exist in this system that enable speakers to judge correctness or incorrectness of utterances. The goal of linguistics, according to Saussure, was to identify the system or structure that underlies instances of speech. He introduced the term *langue* to refer to knowledge of a linguistic system that exists in the mind of a speaker. Langue "was both a social product of the faculty of speech and a collection of necessary conventions that have been adopted by a social body to permit individuals to exercise that faculty" ("Nature" 22). *Parole* represented an instance of language used by a speaker.

According to Saussure, the system of a language consists of *signs* that are available to speakers. Each sign contains two parts: the *signifier,* or form, and the *signified*, or meaning referred to by the signifier. Saussure noted, "The linguistic sign unites, not a thing and a name, but a concept and a sound image. The latter is not the material sound, a purely physical thing, but the psychological imprint of the sound, the impression that it makes on our senses" ("Nature" 26). Signifiers are generally arbitrary, so that Spanish *perro* and English *dog* can both refer to canines.

Each sign in a language exists alongside other signs. A sign gains meaning not in isolation but from features that distinguish it from other signs in the system. Saussure compared language to a game of chess. When taken in isolation, a piece has no meaning. Yet on a chessboard, movement of any piece has implications for all the other pieces on the board.

At times, later linguists challenged Saussure's beliefs. For example, while he saw the interrelatedness of language components as critical, Saussure did not lend importance to context, such as social or formative factors. Sociolinguists later found neglect of these areas to result in a narrow, incomplete view of language (Hymes; Labov, *Sociolinguistics*). While Saussure was content to describe languages, Noam Chomsky would later take issue with Saussure's belief in the adequacy of description as the primary objective of linguistics. Yet overall, Saussure remains a towering figure in the history of the field. Contemporary linguistics retains some of the core ideas from his program.

Saussure's characterization of signs and signifiers led to the work of Charles Sanders Pierce, who founded the discipline of semiotics to interrogate the nature of the relationship between a signifier and the object it represents (Saeed). Pierce, an American, identified distinctive characteristics of three types of signifiers. An *icon* attempts to verbally represent its referent. A photograph of a rose, for instance, is meant to be a visual representation of a rose. *Symbols* are arbitrary forms that are linked to their referents only by convention. Aside from onomatopoeia, words are generally symbols. The third type of signifier in Pierce's approach is the *index*. An index is a type of signifier that is closely connected to its referent, often through causality. For example, the scent of a rose indexes the presence of a rose.

Indexicality features prominently in some contemporary sociolinguistic research, where its function is often colored by ideology. Through repeated use in a particular context, a feature of grammar, lexicon, or phonology comes to be associated with a specific trait. That trait is then assumed to characterize members of a group who use that feature (Ochs; Rahman, "An *ay* for an *ah*" and "The N Word"). For example, *-a* for *-er*, expressed in *eva* for *ever*, was traditionally associated with New Yorkers and, more recently, the Jersey Shore. When associated with New Yorkers, the *-a* ending represented affiliation with the lower social classes (Labov, *Social Stratification*; Lippi-Green).

A problem with indexicality is that the perceived information a feature carries can invite listeners to make judgments of people's worth. For many Americans, a British accent conveys sophistication (Wolfram and Schilling). On the other hand, Appalachian *a*-prefixing, as in *he went a-hunting*, may carry negative associations, casting its users as speakers of a broken code. Yet *a*-prefixing occurs in restricted linguistic environments, according to a complex set of rules governing Appalachian English (Wolfram and Schilling).

Work at the beginning of the twentieth century influenced Leonard Bloomfield, who became known as one of the founders of American structuralism. At that time, many Native American languages faced extinction. Language scholars were working hard to write descriptions of these languages before they vanished. As the anthropologist Franz Boas pointed out, "The position of the natives of America among the races of mankind came to be of considerable interest" (378–79). Studying their languages could potentially yield information about "their origins and relationships" (378–79). Largely to accommodate the academic trend, Bloomfield dedicated himself to attempting to develop a rigorous methodology for recording the features of languages.

Bloomfield was influenced by stimulus-response behaviorism, which means he understood learning as a process of conditioning in which particular stimuli bring specific responses. In this view, children learn language through habits formed from imitation. TESOL methods at the time were grounded in principles of behaviorism. In 1933, Bloomfield published *Language* in which he advocated studying languages by proceeding through levels beginning with sounds, the smallest units of language. Ideally, research would progress to morphology and syntax, with each level studied independently. In reality, Bloomfield focused primarily on phonology and morphology. As a proponent of behaviorism, Bloomfield did not believe it was possible to study meaning scientifically.

Bloomfield differed from Saussure in his regard for social factors that influence the way speakers construct language. He foreshadowed sociolinguistics when he introduced ideas related to the speech community, described as simply "a group of people who interact by means of speech" and share linguistic norms, though their varied ways of speaking may not reflect this ("Speech Communities" 261). While Bloomfield acknowledged linguistic differences based on social class, region, and the presence of Native American and Spanish-speaking communities, he did not give attention to highly stigmatized varieties of English spoken by marginalized groups.

It would take several decades for linguists influenced by the civil rights movement to begin to write about AAE, Hispanic English, and other varieties spoken by groups who were victims of intense discrimination. An exception is Lorenzo Dow Turner's 1930s work among African Americans of the Sea Islands. Turner's research was, at least in part, a response to misrepresentations of the Sapir-Whorf hypothesis that added to an already existing bias against descendants of African people and their language.

Like Bloomfield, Edward Sapir advocated for a structuralist approach to studying language. Influenced by the tenor of his day, Sapir granted that "the languages of a primitive linguistic stock" were amenable to the same methods of analysis as the languages of "more cultured people" (396). Unlike Bloomfield, Sapir was interested in exploring the linguistic implications for sociocultural contexts. The following statement from Sapir summarizes his views: "The real world is to a large extent unconsciously built upon the language habits of the group. No two languages are ever sufficiently similar to be considered as representing the same social reality. The worlds in which different societies live are distinct worlds, not merely the same world with different labels attached" (397).

Benjamin Lee Whorf, a student of Sapir, built on his teacher's work, further developing the hypothesis that the structure of language influences the way speakers perceive and function in the world. In this view, languages have set categories that give structure to the world and enable their speakers to think and reason. According to Whorf, "Formulation of ideas is not an independent process. We dissect nature along lines laid down by our native languages" (117). Structural categories and their contents are not universal but vary from language to language. The distinctiveness of these categories results in different ways of seeing the world; the richness of the categories in a language, in this perception, can affect the depth of intellectual experience that characterizes its speakers.

Sapir's and Whorf's views found expression in the framework of linguistic relativity, which leads humans to interpret the world based on the linguistic system they carry. Neither Sapir nor Whorf favored a deterministic view in which people are unable to transcend limitations imposed by their language. Yet their hypothesis could foster potentially dangerous thinking. Under a deterministic interpretation of Sapir-Whorf, a group's capacity for intellectual engagement can be severely limited by a deficient language.

Such a view would be damaging for African Americans, who were struggling to attain some semblance of fairness in America. Since the transatlantic slave trade began, blacks in America had been victims of an ideology that erased their history and accomplishments, painting them as primitive beings. The language they developed was regarded as crude.

In describing descendants of slaves who made their homes on the Sea Islands and along coastal South Carolina and Georgia, noted scholars of the early 1900s claimed that blacks had no language that was worthy of note. According to Katherine Wyly Mille and Michael B. Montgomery, academics saw Gullah, an African American creole, as "baby talk, the product of impoverished learning capacity. Its speakers were alleged to lack the physical and mental capacity to learn or speak educated English" (xxiii). The scholar A. E. Gonzales wrote the following: "The African brought over or retained only a few words of his jungle-tongue, and even these few are by no means authenticated as part of the original scant baggage of the negro slaves. . . . They seem to have picked from the mouths of their African brothers not a single jungle word for the enrichment of their own speech" (qtd. in Mille and Montgomery 7).

Attitudes toward African Americans and their language were a motivating factor in the work of Turner, the first African American professionally trained linguist. Turner studied with well-known academics and briefly with Sapir. Having spent time among Gullah speakers of the low country of South Carolina and Georgia, Turner was convinced that scholars who maligned their language had overlooked the depth and complexity of the language African Americans in the region spoke. He believed that much of the structure and vocabulary of Gullah was due to West African influence, so he spent time studying West African languages.

Among speakers of Gullah, Turner found a vibrant linguistic environment and was able to identify 4,000 apparently African words that these African Americans were using every day. Turner also found features of grammar and pronunciation that are common to West African languages. In 1949, he published *Africanisms in the Gullah Dialect*, a body of research that caused the beginning of a shift in attitude toward Diasporan language and, by extension, the language of other stigmatized groups. Yet disdain for African American language and varieties spoken by other marginalized groups remained and is still a part of the body of implicit biases in the minds of many. It was several decades after Turner, when as a response to Noam Chomsky, linguists began to develop methods for examining social factors affecting language use and attitudes toward varieties of language. Dell Hymes and William Labov led in this respect.

## Chomsky and the Cognitive Revolution

In a 1959 critique of work by B. F. Skinner, a leading behavioral psychologist, Chomsky introduced ideas that caused linguists to turn away from the claims of both structuralism and behaviorism. In Chomsky's view, healthy humans are universally endowed with an innate language faculty that enables them to learn language as children without explicit intervention. An inborn Universal Grammar contains essential elements of grammatical structure with parameters that allow variation in the way languages fulfill certain structural requirements. For example, it is a universal principle that an adjective must occur in the noun phrase that it modifies. English follows an adjective-noun sequence, as in *blue chair*, while Spanish follows a noun-adjective sequence, as in *silla azul* (chair blue). In another instance, English shows pronominal subject primarily through *I, you, he, she, it, we,* and *they*. English employs little morphology on a verb, adding *-s* on the third-person singular: *I like; you like; he, she, it likes; we like; they like.* A language like Spanish, on the other hand, has a rich morphological system for showing pronominal subject. Verbs take endings to show person, so pronouns are usually not necessary. *I eat*, for example, is *yo como* or simply *como* while *she eats* is *ella come* or *come*.

Chomsky claimed that previous approaches to studying language were inadequate, since they could not explain how children learn the rules of their first language. He described three levels of adequacy that a grammar could attain: observational, descriptive, and explanatory. An *observationally* adequate grammar derives rules from a given set of data and does not consider possibilities from other data. A *descriptively* adequate grammar, such as that sought by the structuralists, derives rules for a language but offers no explanations for how these rules came to exist.

Chomsky drew on Saussure's concept of *langue* and *parole* when he used the terms *competence* and *performance* to distinguish between what a speaker knows about a language and what is apparent in an utterance. He found a fault with the structuralists in that while they offered rules regarding structure, they provided no explanation for how these rules came to exist. The grammars that structuralists wrote dealt only with data from specific languages as well. For a grammar to be *explanatorily* adequate, it should have predictive power that allows it to generalize, generating all of the structures of a language that native speakers would find acceptable (Chomsky, *Aspects*).

Chomsky purposely excluded consideration of social factors from his theory (Chomsky, *Aspects* 3, and *Current Issues* 59–60; also see Labov, *Sociolinguistic Patterns* 186–87). According to Chomsky,

> Linguistic theory is concerned primarily with an ideal speaker-listener, in a completely homogenous speech community, who knows its language perfectly and is unaffected by such grammatically irrelevant conditions as memory limitations, distractions, shifts of attention and interest, and errors . . . in applying his knowledge of the language in actual performance. (*Aspects* 3)

Despite the limitations of Chomsky's focus, his work influenced or led to the development of all of the subfields of contemporary linguistics.

While Chomsky's focus was on an idealized speaker taken out of a natural context, his approach was still able to contribute to an increased understanding of the systematicity and equality of all languages. The Chomsky theory of generative grammar is the topic of a Capstone course I teach in which students apply Chomskyan theory to English as well as an array of other languages. This course affords an opportunity to show students, through their own findings, that all dialects and languages are logical and rules governed.

## Chomsky Detractors

Chomsky was central in introducing the field of cognitive science to linguistics, but not all accepted his view of how processes involved in producing and comprehending language work. In 1980, the linguist George Lakoff collaborated with the philosopher Mark Johnson to write *Metaphors We Live By*, a volume particularly relevant to an English studies program. Lakoff and Johnson cast aside the traditional view of metaphor as an artistic or figurative device, introducing a cognitive approach to the study of metaphor. They rejected Chomskyan theory on neuroscientific, philosophical, and linguistic grounds, claiming that most of our conceptual system is metaphorical in nature. In Lakoff and Johnson's words, "Metaphor is pervasive in everyday life, not just in language but in thought and action. Our ordinary conceptual system, in terms of which we both think and act, is fundamentally metaphorical in nature. . . . If we are right . . . then what we think, what we experience, and what we do every day is very much a matter of metaphor" (*Metaphors* 4).

Metaphor usually employs concrete entities to facilitate understanding of abstract concepts. In metaphorical conceptualizations, the abstract concept actually *is* a concrete entity. For example, the way people talk about argument shows that American culture conceives argument as *war*. In metaphorical terms, argument actually *is* war. Hence, the following representation: ARGUMENT IS WAR (Lakoff and Johnson, *Metaphors* 4). Expressions speakers produce in their day-to-day interactions show that they hold an unconscious conception of argument as war:

> *His criticisms were right on target.*
> *He shot down all of my arguments.*
> *I demolished his argument.*
> (Lakoff and Johnson, *Metaphors* 4)

Other examples of metaphors that underlie daily speech are *time is a limited resource*, *ideas are food*, and *love is madness*. These metaphors cause speakers to produce metaphoric expressions such as *you need to budget your time*, *we don't need to spoon-feed our students*, and *she drives me out of my mind* (Lakoff and Johnson, *Philosophy* 7–9; 46–47)

In the decades since *Metaphors We Live By* was published, the cognitive approach became an influential path to the study of metaphor. Chomsky also came under fire from those who believed language could not be properly studied without attention to social aspects. Contributions from various sources led to the development, mainly in the 1960s, of a new area of linguistics, sociolinguistics, in which scholars aimed to account for language use by various groups and across the many types of social situations speakers encounter. These include, for example, formal and informal environments.

Dell Hymes was a key detractor of the Chomskyan view of the "idealized speaker" as the proper focus of linguistic studies. Hymes recognized that effective interaction required more than knowledge of grammatical structure. He introduced the concept of communicative competence, which included knowledge of the social and cultural norms necessary for successful communication in various situations. Examples are customs for leave-taking, requesting, and conversational turn-taking. Hymes pointed out that a child who lacked knowledge of rules governing these types of situations would be a "social monster" (75).

William Labov, another critic of Chomsky, noted that utterances speakers find acceptable do not necessarily meet standards for well-formedness, as in the Chomsky model (Labov, *Sociolinguistic Patterns* 124). He advanced the notion that an adequate theory of language must acknowledge the variation that exists in the speech of social groups and of individuals. For sociolinguists, variation refers to different ways of expressing the same idea. Variation may be related to factors such as region, age, ethnicity, gender, class, or social conditions. Speech of different groups is often characterized by distinctive features of pronunciation, vocabulary, and grammar. For example, depending largely on the region of a speaker, a long sandwich filled with meat and vegetables may be called a hoagie, submarine, grinder, or hero.

## Variationist Sociolinguistics

Dissatisfaction with the Chomskyan view led Labov to develop a variationist approach, which allows researchers to scientifically study syntactic, phonological, and lexical features as they vary with context. Focusing mainly on group affiliations, his set of methods grew to become the most widely occurring research tradition in sociolinguistics. Labov "established that stylistic variation constitutes a crucial nexus between the individual and the community, between the linguistic, the cognitive, and the social" (Rickford and Eckert 2). Labov began to develop his approach in studies he conducted among residents in Martha's Vineyard, among African American boys in Harlem, among sales clerks in New York City department stores, and among residents of New York's Lower East Side. Variationist methods produce quantitative information based on relatively large amounts of observed data. Finding relative frequency is one method Labov developed to uncover information about factors influencing occurrence of features.

Consider as an example Labov's early work in Martha's Vineyard, an island off the coast of New England. Community norms in Martha's Vineyard allowed choices in producing the vowel sound in words such as *tight* and *ride*. Following pronunciation associated with the mainstream establishment, some speakers produced the vowel sound in these words as *ay* or a rapid *ah-ee*. Other community members produced a local pronunciation that sounds like *uh-ee*, a combination of the vowel sounds in *just* and *seem*. *Tight* for them sounded like *tuh-eet*. Part of Labov's research sought to discover social patterns in use of the *uh-ee* sound. Results show a complex relationship between age, social standing, and attitudes with a tendency to give a local pronunciation to the sound. Table 1.1 shows how age groupings affected the tendency to use the feature.

Labov focused primarily on language as an expression of group membership, but language style also varies within a single speaker. Intraspeaker variation may result from shifts in topic, attitude or mood, and addressee. Shifting styles entails calling on

TABLE **1.1.** Centralization of *ay* in Martha's Vineyard Study

| Age | Score |
|---|---|
| 75+ | 25 |
| 61–75 | 35 |
| 46–60 | 62 |
| 31–45 | 81 |
| 14–30 | 37 |

sets of socially meaningful features that allow a speaker to construct different aspects of identity. As speakers go through their ordinary affairs, they may shift styles, often without conscious awareness. As their styles shift, they express personae representative of various aspects of identity. A student who makes a presentation in class, eats with dining hall mates, and talks with a centenarian great-grandmother likely deploys a different style and persona for each of these situations.

John Rickford and Faye McNair-Knox led in revealing the value of studying variation at the intraspeaker level. At a time when sociolinguistics placed heavy emphasis on dialects and interspeaker variation, Rickford and McNair-Knox demonstrated through quantitative and qualitative methods how addressee and topic can be critical factors in determining the style, and hence persona, that an interviewee presents in a given situation. In a series of interviews researchers conducted with a young African American woman, the interviewee deployed salient linguistic features to create styles representative of two aspects of her identity. In talking to a white interviewer whom she did not know, the interviewee displayed features associated with mainstream "white" English, while she employed features of AAE in talking to an African American interviewer whom she knew. Qualitative analysis suggested that topic also contributed to deployment of features. In analyzing features of AAE as a symbol of identity within a single speaker, Rickford and McNair-Knox were expanding on work done by Rickford's teacher, William Labov.

## African American English

Systematic study of AAE began with research Labov conducted among African American adolescent boys in Harlem. He began his studies because in the 1960s, many African American children in New York City faced challenges in learning to read. A belief prevailed among educators that in order to read, a child needed to command some linguistic system. Following Basil Bernstein ("Language" and *Class*) and reminiscent of earlier scholars who saw African Americans as linguistically deficient, educators took a dim view of African American children's potential to learn. Almost all of these educators were white with no background experience with African Americans, but they believed that African American children had no language.

Labov saw the reading problem as the result of living in a racially stratified system rather than as a consequence of linguistic deficit. He undertook a research program in Harlem that began to uncover the logic and systematicity of AAE. His quantitative research revealed that, far from having no language, the children had command of a linguistically rich code. Labov concluded that "the major causes of reading failure are political and cultural conflicts in the classroom, and dialect differences are important because they are symbols of this conflict" (*Language* xiv).

Children of other underprivileged communities faced learning problems similar to those of the children in Labov's research. He perceived similar causes for their learning difficulties. Specifically, he cited "Puerto Rican and Mexican children from Spanish-speaking homes . . . and the problem of white youth from Appalachian backgrounds and other underprivileged areas" (*Language* 6). Labov presented his views at a meeting of the National Council of Teachers of English. His presentation "addressed squarely the most critical problem: in what way can an understanding of structural differences between [AAVE] and the standard language help teachers of reading" (*Language* 3). Labov's research was conducted among youth who spoke a vernacular variety of AAE.

Increasingly, African American students command language and reading skills that are indistinguishable from those of other students. African Americans may also be proficient in a more mainstream style of ethnic English. Middle-class African Americans, for instance, often employ a style of speech that contains mainstream features of grammar in conjunction with distinctively African American features of pronunciation. This style allows them to express acquiescence to establishment expectations while simultaneously expressing their African American identity (Rahman, "Middle-Class"). Over the course of a few decades, Labov and others, including John Rickford, Russell Rickford, and Baugh, uncovered a range of features, so there is now a fairly complete description of the grammar of African American Vernacular English (AAVE). Understanding how AAVE works can be useful to those preparing to be English teachers as well as others in English studies programs. It is an excellent heuristic tool for teaching principles of linguistics, especially acquisition. Engaging with the structure of AAVE also reveals the logic of this variety, helping to dispel stereotypes. As Labov points out, linguists have learned a great deal about the nature of language through AAE (Labov, *Language*). By extension, this broadens tolerance and acceptance of other stigmatized varieties. Below I describe some of the features of AAVE.

Some of the grammatical features of AAVE occur in other nonstandard varieties. In some cases, grammatical forms and other elements of AAVE vocabulary seem familiar, but they carry meanings that differ from those of General American English (GAE). There are historical reasons for this, often related to the difficult circumstances under which AAVE originated. Features of West African languages and Caribbean Creoles are strong influences in the ethnic language of the African American community. Yet misunderstandings surround the use of words that are familiar in form while conveying unfamiliar meanings. These errors in understanding can contribute to stereotyping and the perception that AAVE is broken English.

*Ain't* is an example. While it is currently in all cases a nonstandard form, in General Non-Standard (GNS) English, this term can be used with all subject pronouns to mean am not, isn't, don't, hasn't, and haven't. Yet in AAVE, ain't can also mean didn't. The following sentence from Rickford and Rickford (123) illustrates this use:

> He ain't go no [= didn't go any] further than third or fourth grade.

Negative concord in AAVE bears some similarity to double negatives, such as GNS *he ain't got none.* A difference is that it negates auxiliary verbs and all indefinite pronouns in a sentence, as in the following. The AAVE sentence also shows that a negative auxiliary can head a sentence with a following negative:

> AAVE: Can't nobody make none.
> GAE: Nobody can make any.

In several constructions, *-s* may be absent in AAVE where it is present in GAE. Genitive possessives in GAE require *-s* as an ending, as in *Sally's car*. African American Vernacular English removes the *-s* ending, as in the expression *baby momma*, which refers to the mother of a man's child.

In GAE, third-person singular verbs add *-s* to the end, as in *she runs*. African American Vernacular English levels verb forms: subjects are mandatory, and *-s* is not needed, since it provides information already present in the subject. In the sentence below, it is clear from the pronoun that the subject is third-person singular: *She run*. This sentence is acceptable in AAVE.

Where GAE uses *-s* to show plural, AAVE does not require it where there is a quantifier modifier, as in *five chair*. A number of modifiers such as *many* and *some* show that a noun is plural, so that *-s* is redundant: it does not add meaning. The name of the rapper 50 Cent illustrates AAVE's absence of plural *-s*.

Another grammatical feature of AAVE is the existential *it*. A principle of Chomskyan grammar posits that every sentence, in every language, must have a subject. As I have noted, parameters often exist for fulfilling universal linguistic requirements. In the sentence *There's a fly in my soup*, *there* has no meaning; the sentence has no subject with semantic content. *There* is a dummy subject, present in the sentence to fulfill the requirement that every sentence must have a subject. African American Vernacular English selects a different word for filling the subject slot. In the following AAVE sentence, *it* is the dummy subject, serving the same function as *there* in the GAE sentence:

AAVE: It's a fly in my soup.
GAE: There's a fly in my soup.

A compelling component of AAVE is its unique system of tense-aspect markers. Aspect differs from tense in showing how something happens in time rather than when. For example, aspect shows that an event happens continually, sporadically, or slowly. In AAVE, the habitual *be* shows that an event or state occurs continually or habitually. This construction is at the heart of many "Ebonics" jokes, where outsiders assume a sentence like *John be at the store* means *John is at the store.* The sentence actually means *John is usually at the store.*

Another AAVE marker is completive *done. Done* here differs from the *done* generally found in GNS, since it is not a standalone verb. Usually, *done* serves as a main verb, but in AAVE, it can accompany a main verb to show that an action is completely over. Below are examples illustrating *done* as a main verb in GNS and as a completive in AAVE:

GNS: She done her homework.
AAVE: She done washed the dishes.

These are a few features of the grammatical system of AAVE.

There is a host of other factors that makes the dialect work. In AAVE, the copula may be absent in most present-tense constructions. There are languages such as Russian that do not employ a copula equivalent to *be.* An example is *He tall.* Circumstances for every variety are different, but each has rules to govern structures that may seem odd to outsiders.

Along with understanding something of the grammatical structure of AAVE, it is useful to know that African Americans have made significant contributions to the American lexicon. *Bling*, meaning flashy jewelry; *24/7*, meaning constantly; and *sassy* are examples (Rahman, *N Word*). Quite a few words that have crossed over from the African American lexicon to the mainstream are words captives brought from Africa. *Tote* and *Bambi*, for example, are from African words meaning carry and the place where a baby antelope lies down to hide (Holloway; Rahman, *N Word*).

Most quantitative work has addressed issues in grammar and phonology, but occasionally, words or expressions become subjects of quantitative analysis. In 2012, I published the first linguistic inquiry into use of the term *nigga* among African Americans. I held intuitions about the subject prior to researching it, but my objective was to learn through statistical methods who was most likely to use the term and under what circumstances. African American English offers a range of terms for group self-reference, so above all, I wanted to know why speakers would employ a seemingly pejorative term to refer to themselves.

I chose for data collection the work of successful, socially conscious African American comedians who perform before primarily African American audiences. These professionals are an important repository of African American cultural knowledge and a gauge of ideas that circulate within the community. While their performances appear spontaneous, they are carefully crafted in advance of presentation. The effective comedians share with their audiences a metapragmatic understanding of the semiotic value of linguistic features. This knowledge has developed from past community uses of features in contexts they recognize (Rahman, "An *ay* for an *ah*" and "The N Word"). The comedians' awareness allows them to effectively deploy salient linguistic features as resources.

Results in the statistical study suggest that *nigga* is unlike other African American ethnonyms, such as *blood*, *brother*, and *sister* (Rahman, "Woman to Woman" and "The N Word"). While these terms all suggest identity and solidarity with the African American community, *nigga* specifically draws meaning from the four-hundred-year struggle of African Americans to survive the harsh experience of slavery and its aftermath. Use of the term identifies a speaker as participating in a culture of survival. Addressing or referring to another African American as *nigga* generally marks that person as a co-participant in the culture. *Nigga* is presently seen as a variant of *nigger*, which is used as a racist epithet. I am presently completing a book that traces the origin and development of the two as symbolic terms.

The following examples from successful African American comedians feature *nigga* in contexts that show African Americans as survivors. In the first instance, Freeze Love describes a hypothetical scene where lights go out in a theater where he is performing. Love's statement alludes to the survival skills of African Americans:

> Freeze Love: All of us niggas will make it out of here safe and sound. We niggas.

In the second instance, Katt Williams refers to an African American ability to survive hardship:

> Katt Williams: I'm proud of niggas. Niggas don't never quit. Niggas always come through the motherfuckin' trouble—and looking better at the same time.

*Nigga* may also convey negative meaning. At times, it is used as a reprimand to show that an African American has behaved in a way that does not meet the standards of the African American community. In these cases, *nigga* is an ironic reference to the racist term *nigger*. An African American has behaved the way that biased whites say niggers behave (Rahman, "Woman to Woman" and "The N Word").

## Results of Variationist Research

Survival findings in *N*-word research were based on statistical (quantitative) analysis, but sociolinguists may also employ qualitative methods to explore any of the range of societal issues that concern linguists. A vibrant tradition of qualitative research has arisen around the topic of gender. In 1973, Robin Lakoff published a paper in which she identified a style she called "women's language." Lakoff suggested that because of societal constraints placed on women, they were forced to produce speech that reflected and reinforced an identity based on helplessness and acquiescence to males. Women's language was characterized by a large vocabulary related to domestic activities; "empty" adjectives, such as *divine* and *charming*; and hedges that show uncertainty, such as *well* and *kinda* (Robin Lakoff).

Critics saw Robin Lakoff's work as narrow in its focus, since it took as its model the language of white, upper-middle-class women. Researchers have challenged the suggestion that the linguistic behavior of middle-class white women is representative of the practices of women as a group (Cameron; Philips; Talbot). The work was, by Robin Lakoff's admission, largely impressionistic and anecdotal. In a 2010 interview with Catherine E. Davies, Robin Lakoff comments that at the time of her early work, she was "unaware of the multiple ambiguities present in most forms of utterance" (Davies 372). Yet Robin Lakoff's work paved the way for subsequent work in an area that had received little attention. Studies in language and gender have proliferated in recent decades, addressing myriad issues. There has been a movement toward studying gendered language in context. Additionally, newer research attends to gendered language among diverse groups (see, for example, Kiesling; Mendoza-Denton; Rahman, "Woman to Woman").

## Spoken Language

So far, the discussion has focused on spoken language. Bloomfield expressed an extreme position regarding written language when he stated that, "writing is not language, but merely a way of recording language by means of visible marks" (*Language* 21) Most contemporary linguists understand that both spoken and written language reflect linguistic competence, but they also believe spoken language is a more direct expression of the processes that underlie speech production. As F. Coulmas points out, "writing is not just visible speech, but rather a mode of verbal communication in its own right" (12).

Linguists may, in some instances, see reason to analyze written texts. This has become increasingly the case in recent decades. The sociolinguist Gretchen McCullough is interested, for instance, in identifying linguistic constructions in social media and the ways in which such media are influencing both spoken and written language. In areas such as historical linguistics, most data have necessarily always been written.

Still, most work in linguistics focuses on spoken language, which can provide a window for observing competence as it emerges in a child. Many linguists are interested in this process of language learning and its social and structural outcomes. Writing, on the other hand, derives from spoken language; it is always the result of teaching. In spoken language, speakers usually have an audience that is physically present, and they often adjust their speech in response to verbal and subtle nonverbal cues they receive from listeners. The features they select, generally without conscious awareness, are often imbued with social meaning. Since the language is spoken, the shifts may include pronunciation. A linguist can study these shifts, especially in pronunciation, in ways not possible with written texts.

For a precise picture of vocal sounds, linguists may conduct spectrographic analysis. This procedure can provide specific measurements of aspects of a sound, such as pitch, loudness, durations of sound, and speed of speech. These are all qualities that can contribute to the semiotic value of a spoken expression. Spectrographic analysis can, for example, capture details of vocal fry, a low, creaky sound created by a slow vibration of the vocal chords. Scholars have noted use of this feature in various social groups, including Latinx communities and college-aged women (Fought; Gottliebson, Lee, Weinrich, and Sanders; Mendoza-Denton; Yuasa).

The world is becoming increasingly open to accepting nontraditional genres as literature and as texts. Bob Dylan, for instance, received a Nobel Prize for literature. Hip-hop artists such as Nas and Public Enemy have publicly discussed the process of creating raps that have merit. These artists and younger ones such as Kendrick Lamar have produced work that can benefit humanity. Their works are worthy of attention in English studies.

In the introduction to this volume, Bruce McComiskey points to a need for English studies to expand its notion of what counts as texts. He states, "Texts are not just words on pages; they are any semiotic mode on or in any medium." Broadening the meaning of text allows for sanctioning of verbal performances including work by comedians. Here, pronunciation of vowels and consonants as well as prosodic features like intonation, stress, and amplitude can all become analyzable as part of a text. The same is true of recorded spontaneous speech from interviews and conversations among consultants.

Ordinary interactions involve the projection of personae, but these are not usually conscious performances. Investigating spoken texts from genres of popular culture such as hip-hop and stand-up comedy entails looking into the purposeful use of features to construct personae in overt public performances. Socially conscious performances offer a number of insights into linguistics, cultural norms, and societal attitudes.

Observing the structure of contemporary artists' works allows students to analyze language in contexts that explicitly convey social meanings and aspects of identity. Additionally, investigating spoken texts may introduce students to unfamiliar varieties of English. Students understand that Standard English is appropriate for many environments, but examining diverse types of English opens opportunities for learning about the systematicity of all language varieties and contributions groups have made to the English language. A short excerpt from the hip-hop artist Kendrick Lamar provides a simple example. Lamar employs features of AAVE throughout his body of work. This enhances his identity as an African American hip-hop artist. In "Alright," Lamar says the following:

> We gon' be alright.
> Do you hear me, do you feel me?

A rule of AAVE influences his pronunciation of *alright*. To explain, I should note that linguists are concerned with the sounds we hear rather than those suggested by orthographic spelling. According to the AAE rule, the *ay* sound in *right* can be pronounced *ah* when it occurs before voiced consonants (*b*, *d*, *g*, *j*, *l*, *m*, *n*, *r*, *v*, *w*, *z*) or at the end of a word. Before voiceless consonants (*p*, *t*, *f*, *k*, *and s*), the rule requires speakers to produce *ay*. The sound we hear after the vowel in *right* is *t*, so the rule calls for *rayt*, rather than *raht*. Consistent with the rule, Lamar produces *rayt*.

Figurative language is prominent in the work of hip-hop artists. In the segment above, *do you feel me?* is a metaphorical expression from an underlying metaphor of AAE: conveying knowledge is touching someone. The preceding question, *Do you hear me?* is similarly a metaphorical expression from a related system where conveying knowledge is being audible.

A part of my research has involved investigating comedians' spoken texts (Rahman, "African American Divas," "An *ay* for an *ah*," and "Woman to Woman"). The article "An *ay* for an *ah*" explores the conscious and purposeful projection of personae by a group of well-known African American comedians. The research examines fifteen narratives by DL Hughley, Adele Givens, Steve Harvey, and other comedians as they construct characters representative of African Americans and groups of whites. Based on qualitative analysis of attitudes and behaviors of the characters, I placed them into a group consisting of five factors: middle-class establishment; African American narrator; ethnic Italian; African American non-narrator; and middle-class African American narrator.

Comedians have but short spaces of time to construct their characters. They have no costumes, props, or sets to help them to transition from one character to another, so an area of interest is how they use language to perform the character shifts. The features they deploy must have indexical power sufficient to draw contrasts that will allow audiences to quickly recognize characters as African American or as members of the middle-class establishment or other group. The dipthongal variant *ay* is associated with the northern middle class and the monophthongal variant *ah* with ethnic speech of the African American community (Labov, *Language*; Rickford, 1999; Rahman, "An *ay* for an *ah*" and "Middle-Class"). I wanted to see how these variants would play out in the comedians' narratives. Most specifically, I was interested in determining whether group membership of the character or some other factor was the strongest predictor of occurrences of *ay*.

To find out whether character role, type of phrase, gender of character, or following sound most favored the occurrence of *ay*, I conducted a regression analysis of the 446 instances where *ay* or *ah* could occur in the data.

Varbrul is a computer program for statistical analysis that calculates factor weights showing "the extent to which a combination of factors independently and simultaneously constrain the occurrence of a particular feature" (Paolillo). On a scale of 0 to 1.0, Varbrul can measure factors favoring or disfavoring application of a feature. Weights over .500 favor implementation while weights under .500 disfavor it (Paolillo). Table 1.2 shows results of the Varbul process for the analysis of *ay*.

Factor Group 1 consists of character roles, while Factor Group 2 consists of instances when the topic of an utterance reveals a focus on logic or analysis regardless of who the character is. It turns out these groups are the only significant influences on

TABLE 1.2. Results of Varbrul Regression Analysis Procedure for [*ay*]

| | Relatives Frequency of [*ay*] | Weight |
|---|---|---|
| Factor Group 1: Role | | |
| Middle-class establishment | 52/62 | .952 |
| Middle-class African American narrator | 18/28 | .781 |
| Ethnic Italian | 29/46 | .750 |
| African American narrator | 32/237 | .326 |
| African American character | 5/73 | .203 |
| Range .749 | | |
| Factor Group 2: Phrase | | |
| Analytical thinking | 28/34 | .917 |
| Not specifically related to analytical thinking | 108/412 | [.451] |
| Range. 466 | | |
| Factor Group 3: Gender of Characters | | |
| Male | 111/334 | .524 |
| Female | 25/112 | [.430] |
| Range .094 | | |
| Factor Group 4: Following Phonological Environment | | |
| Nasal | 20/62 | .534 |
| Voiced | 22/85 | .508 |
| # | 94/299 | [.491] |
| Range .043 | | |
| Total | 136/446 | |

occurrences of *ay*. The input probability of .255 means that *ay* is likely to occur at a rate of approximately 25 percent as opposed to *ah*. Role is the leading factor group for explaining its occurrence. The high weight for middle-class establishment compared to the low weights for African American characters shows that even though AAVE rules require *ay* in some environments, *ay* is far more likely to occur in portrayals of the middle-class establishment than in portrayals of working-class African Americans. The monophthong *ah* occurs with a range of phonological and grammatical features of AAVE that help to establish identity and solidarity with the African American community. This is consistent with research that associates the sounds with the two groups (Labov; Rahman, "Middle-Class").

The overall message in the narratives is self-empowering to the African American community. At the expense of the middle-class establishment, the comedians portray African Americans as "culturally rich survivors," resilient, resourceful, and able to "make a way where there is no way" (Rahman, "An *ay* for an *ah*"). The comedians place the characters into situations where their attitudes and behaviors indicate the traits indexed by the linguistic features. They depict the middle-class establishment as exaggerated embodiments of an establishment ideology that casts them as slavishly conservative, naïve, reliant on a "by-the-book" logic, to the total detriment of common sense and feelings. Table 1.3 compares traits scholars associate with the middle-class establishment with their hyperbolic expression in the narratives.

Middle-class people appear as reserved and unassertive with a deep loyalty to societal institutions and especially to one's employer. According to Kanter, establishment ideology tells adherents that this loyalty will lead to lifelong social and economic

TABLE **1.3.** Middle-Class Traits and Their Expressions in Comedic Narratives

| **Traits Ascribed to the Middle-Class Establishment (Kanter; Eckert)** | **Possible Hyperbolic Expressions of Middle-Class Traits in Narratives** |
|---|---|
| Forsaking local and regional affiliations | Culturally unaware, ethnically bland |
| Ruled by logic and reason | Foolishly pragmatic |
| Conservative | Slavishly conservative |
| "Rule-minded" | Functioning with "manual in hand" |
| Use of SE; avoidance of faddish language | Stilted speech; outmoded slang, interjections |
| Impersonal, dispassionate in interactions | Stiff, rigid in interactions |
| Team player | Martyr |
| Naïve | Extremely naïve; gullible |
| Smooth, personal style | Carefully rehearsed "casual" style |

security. According to Steve Harvey, "When you fire white people, they don't ever see it coming." When a Steve Harvey white establishment character is fired, he is at first in disbelief: "What're you talking about?" Then, in a state of shock, he breaks down and weakly appeals to his boss: "For Pete's sake! Oh, Tom, what am I going to do? What about the mortgage? What about the children's college fund? Oh, Father God!"

By contrast to the middle class, the self-empowering pragmatism of African Americans comes through when an African American DL Hughley character is fired. Employing *ah* and other features of AAVE, the Hughley character says,

> How come you didn't call me at home, mothafucka? You knew I was fired yesterday! Making me burn up all my goddamn gas! (2000)

The research suggests a relationship between the middle class-establishment and emphasis on analysis and logic, but utterances showing exercise of logic may occur independently of character role (Rahman, "An *ay* for an *ah*").

Factor Group 2 analyzes the likelihood that *ay* will occur in utterances that show analytical thinking, regardless of character. This Factor Group is independent of Factor Group 1 yet related because the middle-class establishment is ideologically associated with logic and analytical thinking. Still, the middle class alone is not responsible for the strong prediction. While African American characters use features of AAVE intensively, they call on *ay* in statements that reflect an analytical stance. Below are a few utterances from African American characters that foreground analytical thinking. Italics show words suggesting a thoughtful or analytical stance.

> Eddie Murphy: I *read* a whole bunch of Hallmark cards.
> Steve Harvey: It's *denial.*
> Richard Pryor: I *know* what's next after "yee-haw."
> Adele Givens: I am so glad y'all *decided* to join me.

Rules of AAE allow *ay* in certain linguistic environments but not the ones above. Yet the comedians employ the *ay* variant in the words *I*, *denial*, and *decided*. Beyond indicating affiliation with the middle-class establishment, the *ay* diphthong appears to index traits associated with logic. This may be true across social groups in America; in that case, the feature is available to anyone as a tool for constructing a relevant aspect of identity.

## Conclusion

In the introduction to this volume, Bruce McComiskey offers that for English studies to flourish in the twenty-first century, it will have to see itself as a process rather than as a static entity. This will allow it to adopt a more global, cosmopolitan view that is better able to fold into its curricular model linguistics and other areas that have traditionally stood at the periphery of activity in English studies. Acceptance of change as natural and potentially evolutionary movement creates an intellectual environment that is less encumbered by the past and more receptive to new approaches. McComiskey's proposal to expand notions of what English studies encompasses, which I discussed earlier, illustrates the type of change that will benefit English studies.

Principles McComiskey sets forth for the evolution of English studies also attend to the need of scholars to engage with the public. The relevance of sociolinguistics to events in the world occasionally brings sociolinguists into contact with the public. In recent decades, linguistics has evolved so that it acknowledges the validity of nonstandard varieties as organized systems of communication that convey social meaning for users. Without minimizing the importance of speech considered standard, sociolinguists have also been foremost in seeking to end language discrimination.

John Rickford has written in several media outlets about the impact of language discrimination in the trial of George Zimmerman. Zimmerman stood trial for the murder of Trayvon Martin, an African American adolescent. Rachel Jeantel, Martin's close friend, was talking to him by cell phone at the time of his death. When Jeantel took the witness stand at the trial, she employed features of AAE. The jury rejected her testimony, claiming that her speech was incomprehensible.

I have written blogs and done a number of media interviews on topics related to the *N* word and various other language issues related to African Americans. I worked with Housing Opportunities Made Equal (HOME) in addressing a widespread phenomenon in which people become victims of discrimination based on the sound of their voices on the telephone. This may occur where callers are perceived as Latinx, LGTBQ, African American, elderly, disabled, or a member of a number of marginalized groups. People habitually make judgments of others based on the sound of their voices. They do this after hearing segments of speech as short as twenty-eight seconds (Rahman, "Middle-Class").

Academic institutions will have to find ways to acknowledge public scholarship since one of the greatest values in creating knowledge is in being able to make it available for people to use. Along with that, universities will need to devise methods of ensuring that significant substance is not lost, even as work is framed for general audiences.

While this chapter focuses on sociolinguistics, other branches of linguistics can contribute significantly to an English studies program. For instance, in this technologically driven globalized world, words are being constantly added to the English lexicon. This often happens by manipulating parts of old words. Morphologists, who study word formation, can add insight to understanding processes by which speakers create words; a course that covers morphology can contribute to a broadened view, since words that enter the twenty-first century vocabulary often arise from technology or from other languages.

Branches of linguistics continue to emerge and grow. An example is computational linguistics, which involves attempting to automate language-processing tasks. Biolinguistics delves into the Universal Grammar, attempting to determine the extent to which language is acquired rather than innate. It is impossible to know where linguistics will move next, but it has changed dramatically over the last one hundred years. Based on knowledge that is now available, future changes will likely continue to confirm the value of linguistics to the field of English studies.

## Works Cited

Baugh, John. *Black Street Speech: Its History, Structure, and Survival.* U of Texas P, 1983.

———. *Out of the Mouths of Slaves: African American Language and Educational Malpractice.* U of Texas P, 1999.

Bernstein, Basil. *Class, Codes, and Control.* Vol. 1, Routledge, 1971.

———. "Social Class, Language and Socialization." *The Routledge Language and Cultural Theory Reader*, edited by Lucy Burke, Tony Crowley, and Alan Girvin, Routledge, 2000, pp. 448–55.

———. "Language and Social Class." *Butoh Journal of Sociology*, vol. 10, 1960, pp. 311–26.

Bloomfield, Leonard. *Language.* George Allen & Unwin, 1933.

———. "Speech Communities." *The Routledge Language and Cultural Theory Reader*, edited by Lucy Burke, Tony Crowley, and Alan Girvin, Routledge, 2000, pp. 261–68.

Boas, Franz. "Race and Language." *The Routledge Language and Cultural Theory Reader*, edited by Lucy Burke, Tony Crowley, and Alan Girvin, Routledge, 2000, pp. 378–85.

Bourdieu, Pierre. "The Production and Reproduction of Legitimate Language." *The Routledge Language and Cultural Theory Reader*, edited by Lucy Burke, Tony Crowley, and Alan Girvin, Routledge, 2000, pp. 467–77.

Cameron, Deborah. "Introduction." *The Feminist Critique of Language: A Reader,* edited by Deborah Cameron, Routledge, 1998, pp. 3–12.

Chomsky, Noam. *Aspects of the Theory of Syntax.* MIT P, 1965.

———. *Current Issues in Linguistic Theory.* Mouton, 1964.

Coulmas, F. "Language Adaptation." *Language Adaptation*, edited by Florian Coulmas, Cambridge UP, 1989.

Davies, Catherine Evans. "Interview with Robin Tolmach Lakoff." *Journal of English Linguistics*, vol. 38, no. 4, Dec. 2010, pp. 369–76.

Eckert, Penelope. "Style and Social Meaning." *Style and Sociolinguistic Variation*, edited by Penelope Eckert and John R. Rickford, Cambridge UP, 2002, pp. 119–26.

Fought, Carmen. *Chicano English in Context.* Palgrave Macmillan, 2003.

Gottliebson, Renee Ogle, Linda Lee, et al. "Voice Problems of Future Speech-Language Pathologists." *Journal of Voice*, vol. 21, no. 6, Nov. 2007, pp. 699–704.

Holloway, Joseph E. "Africanisms in African American Names in the United States." *Africanisms in American Culture*, 2nd ed., edited by Joseph E. Holloway. Indiana UP, 2005, pp. 18–38.

Hymes, Dell. *Foundations in Sociolinguistics: An Ethnographic Approach.* U of Philadelphia P, 1974.

Jesperson, Otto. *Language: Its Nature, Development and Origins.* Henry Holt and Company, 1922.

Kanter, Rosabeth Moss. *Men and Women of the Corporation.* Basic Books, 1993.

Kendi, Ibram X. *Stamped from the Beginning: The Definitive History of Racist Ideas in America.* Nation Books, 2016.

Kiesling, Scott Fabius. "Prestige, Cultural Models, and Other Ways of Talking about Underlying Norms and Gender." *The Handbook of Language and Gender*, edited by Janet Holmes and Miriam Meyerhoff, Blackwell, 2003, pp. 509–27.

Labov, William. *Language in the Inner City: Studies in the Black English Vernacular.* U of Pennsylvania P, 1972.

———. "The Logic of Non-Standard English." *The Routledge Language and Cultural Theory Reader*, edited by Lucy Burke, Tony Crowley, and Alan Girvin, Routledge, 2000, pp. 456–66.

———. *The Social Stratification of English in New York City.* Center for Applied Linguistics, 1966.

———. *Sociolinguistic Patterns.* U of Pennsylvania P, 1972.

Lakoff, George, and Mark Johnson. *Metaphors We Live By.* U of Chicago P, 1980.

———. *Philosophy in the Flesh: The Embodied Mind and Its Challenge to Western Thought.* Basic Books, 1999.

Lakoff, Robin. "Language and Woman's Place." *Language in Society*, vol. 2, no. 1, Apr. 1973, pp. 45–79.

Lippi-Green, Rosina. *English with an Accent.* Routledge, 1997.

McCulloch, Gretchen. *Because Internet: Understanding the New Rules of Language.* Riverhead, 2019.

Meinhof, Carl. *An Introduction to the Study of African Languages.* J. M. Dent & Sons, 1915.

Mendoza-Denton, Norma. *Homegirls: Language and Cultural Practice among Latina Youth Gangs.* Wiley-Blackwell, 2008.

Mille, Katherine Wyly, and Michael B. Montgomery. *Introduction. Africanisms in the Gullah Dialect.* U of South Carolina P, 2002.

Ochs, Elinor. "Indexing Gender." *Rethinking Context: Language as an Interactive Phenomenon*, edited by Alessandra Duranti and Charles Goodwin. Cambridge UP, 1992, pp. 335–58.

Paolillo, John C. *Analyzing Linguistic Variation: Statistical Models and Methods.* Center for the Study of Language and Information, 2002.

Patrick, Peter L. "Pidgins, Creoles, and Variation." *The Handbook of Pidgin and Creole Studies*, edited by Silvia Kouwenberg and John Victor Singler, Blackwell, 2009, pp. 461–87.

Philips, Susan U. "The Power of Gender Ideologies in Discourse." *The Handbook of Language and Gender*, edited by Janet Holmes and Miriam Meyerhoff, Blackwell, 2003, pp. 252–76.

Rahman, Jacquelyn. "African American Divas of Comedy: Staking a Claim in Public Space." *The Oxford Handbook of African American Language*, edited by Sonja Lanehart, Oxford UP, 2015, pp. 723–39.

———. "An *ay* for an *ah*: Language of Survival in African American Narrative Comedy." *American Speech*, vol. 82, no.1, spring 2007, pp. 65–96.

———. "Middle-Class African Americans: Reactions and Attitudes toward African American English." *American Speech,* vol. 83, no. 2, 2008, pp. 141–76.

———. "The N Word: Its History and Use in the African American Community." *Journal of English Linguistics*, vol. 40, no. 2, 2012, pp. 137–71.

———. *N Word Papers Expose Secrets to Help Heal the Divide*, forthcoming.

———. "Woman to Woman: Building Solidarity in African American Female Comedy." *English World-Wide: A Journal of Varieties of English*, vol. 32, no. 3, 2011, pp. 309–37.

Rickford, John Russell. *African American Vernacular English: Features, Evolution, Educational Implications*. Wiley-Blackwell, 1999.

Rickford, John Russell, and Penelope Eckert. Introduction. *Style and Sociolinguistic Variation*, edited by Penelope Eckert and John Russell Rickford, Cambridge UP, 2002, pp. 1–18.

Rickford, John Russell, and Faye McNair-Knox. "Addressee- and Topic-Influenced Style Shift: A Quantitative Sociolinguistic Study." *Sociolinguistic Perspectives on Register*, edited by Douglas Biber and Edward Finegan, Oxford UP, 1994, pp. 235–76.

Rickford, John Russell, and Russell John Rickford. *Spoken Soul: The Story of Black English*. Wiley & Sons, 2000.

Rickford, John Russell, Julie Sweetland, Angela C. Rickford, and Thomas Grano. *African American, Creole, and other Vernacular Englishes in Education: A Bibliographic Resource*. Routledge, 2013.

Saeed, John I. *Semantics*. Wiley & Sons, 2016.

Sapir, Edward. "The Status of Linguistics as a Science." *The Routledge Language and Cultural Theory Reader*, edited by Lucy Burke, Tony Crowley, and Alan Girvin, Routledge, 2000, pp. 395–400.

Saussure, Ferdinand de. "Language and Linguistics." *The Routledge Language and Cultural Theory Reader*, edited by Lucy Burke, Tony Crowley, and Alan Girvin, Routledge, 2000, pp. 53–63.

———. "Linguistic Value." *The Routledge Language and Cultural Theory Reader*, edited by Lucy Burke, Tony Crowley, and Alan Girvin, Routledge, 2000, pp. 105–113.

———. "The Nature of the Linguistic Sign." *The Routledge Language and Cultural Theory Reader*, edited by Lucy Burke, Tony Crowley, and Alan Girvin, Routledge, 2000, pp. 21–32.

Schneider, Edgar W., editor. *Focus on the U.S.A.* Benjamins, 1996.

Shulz, Muriel R. "The Semantic Derogation of Woman." *The Routledge Language and Cultural Theory Reader*, edited by Lucy Burke, Tony Crowley, and Alan Girvin, Routledge, 2000, pp. 82–91.

Talbot, Mary. "Gender Stereotypes: Reproduction and Challenge." *The Handbook of Language and Gender*, edited by Janet Holmes and Miriam Meyerhoff. Blackwell, 2003, pp. 468–86.

Tamasi, Susan, and Lamont Antieu. *Language and Linguistic Diversity in the US: An Introduction.* Routledge, 2015.

Turner, Lorenzo Dow. *Africanisms in the Gullah Dialect.* U of South Carolina P, 2002.

Whorf, Benjamin Lee. "Science and Linguistics." *The Routledge Language and Cultural Theory Reader*, edited by Lucy Burke, Tony Crowley, and Alan Girvin, Routledge, 2000, pp. 114–21.

Wolfram, Walt, and Natalie Schilling. *American English: Dialects and Variation.* 3rd ed., Wiley & Sons, 2016.

Yuasa, Ikuko P. "Creaky Voice: A New Feminine Voice Quality for Young Urban-Oriented Upwardly Mobile American Women?" *American Speech*, vol. 85, no. 3, 2010, pp. 315–37.

## Media References

Harvey, Steve. Platinum Comedy Series—*Steve Harvey: One Man.* Venture Distribution. 2001.

Hughley, D. L. *The Original Kings of Comedy.* MTV Networks and Latham Entertainment. 2000.

Lamar, Kendrick. "Alright." *To Pimp a Butterfly.* Aftermath/Interscope Records. 2005.

Pryor, Richard. *That Nigger's Crazy.* Partee/Stax. 1974.

Williams, Katt. *It's Pimpin Pimpin.* Salient. 2008.

# *Rhetoric and Composition*

VICTOR VILLANUEVA
*Washington State University, Emeritus*

For most college students, the required first-year composition course is their primary introduction to English studies: learning the ways of writing that tend to be valued in the university and being introduced to the kinds of reading they will likely need to undertake, whether as essays or even as literature in English. And in that first-year composition course, students probably learn that writing is a process. And if they are introduced to rhetoric, it is to ethos, pathos, and logos, and maybe logic or logical fallacies. All that's good. This offers an introduction to two fields that often work together as one in English studies: rhetoric and composition. What makes them two different fields, though they're often invoked as "rhetoric and composition," "composition and rhetoric," or even "rhetoric and writing studies," is historical and a matter of emphasis. But it does take understanding rhetoric—or rhetorics, plural—to be able to understand how best to approach writing.

## Beginnings (or the Official Story)

"Composition" or "Writing Studies" in some ways has a history that goes back to the Roman rhetorician Cicero in the first century BCE (Crowley 50–52). It traces back to him in two ways. First, Cicero was the most noted rhetorician to place emphasis on writing; that was a change. Prior to Cicero, the greater emphasis was on oratory, on speaking. Three centuries before Cicero, for example, Aristotle described inartistic proofs of evidence in rhetoric; in so doing, he placed written contracts just one step above the testimony of slaves under torture (1376b). That's not a great deal of faith in the value of writing and is quite the opposite of our contemporary sensibility to "get it in writing." Aristotle's teacher, Plato, who also wrote quite a bit, actually argued against the viability of writing, which is quite an irony in the dialogue titled *Phaedrus*. Cicero, on the other hand, was given to writing, writing letters every day, and writing works that would be read in Western Europe for centuries: *De Inventione* in Latin or *On Invention* in English (Kennedy, *Classical Rhetoric*). In this case, "invention" meant discovering what one had to say. In that first-year writing course, instructors might have called this "prewriting" or might have instructed students to "freewrite."

Another reason we can trace "comp" back to Cicero is because what we think of as academic discourse, or the patterns of writing that tend to find acceptance in academic circles, finds its roots in Cicero's *On Invention*. Cicero's intention was not to dictate how to write an academic or scientific essay, but that was the effect nevertheless. In fact, clearly his intention was to provide information about how one might proceed in a legal setting. Not only was Cicero an orator, writer, and politician (he was elected to head the Roman Senate as consul in 63 BCE), he was also a lawyer a generation before the emperor Claudius dictated that official lawyers would be paid for their services. Cicero was, in other words, a pioneer among lawyers. If you watch any legal drama on television or in the movies, you will see lawyers giving opening statements to a jury, telling the jury what the lawyers will set out to prove during the trial. They then will call witnesses and question the opposition's witnesses, after which the lawyers will provide closing statements—summaries of what was presented and the implications from that testimony. That same process is that of the academic paper: an intro that says what will follow, the "proofs," considerations of counterarguments, and a closing or conclusion. The model for academic discourse is the system first provided in *De Inventione*, as contemporary scholars of rhetoric and composition have noted (Crowley).

But the first time the exact phrase "composition and rhetoric" was invoked was in a book by nineteenth-century Scottish philosopher Alexander Bain. He titled the book, first published in 1867, *English Composition and Rhetoric: A Manual*. If you were required to write a description paper, a narrative paper, or a persuasive paper, those genres (called "the modes": description, narration, persuasion, exposition, and poetry) were first described by Bain. The source for the modes was faculty psychology, a view of the brain as being almost like muscles: certain parts of the brain address certain functions, and therefore, each part of the brain must be exercised. The modes, then, were not simply genres but were designed to exercise particular parts of the brain (Harned; Crowley).

Composition, in the way we think of it now, was first introduced by Francis James Child, who was a Boylston Professor of Rhetoric and Oratory at Harvard University. Child changed his title from Professor of Rhetoric and Oratory to Professor of English (Harvard's first professor of English) in 1876. He was concerned that incoming students weren't fully prepared to write about literature, so he assigned his teaching assistant the task of preparing first-year students for this task. In a sense, then, 1876 marked the beginning of comp, albeit in the service of English literature (Berlin 22–23).

It wasn't until the 1960s that comp truly began, at least in the fashion students likely experience it now. Well, to be precise, it began in 1959. That's when the National Academy of Sciences sponsored the Woods Hole Conference. The director of that conference was the cognitive psychologist Jerome Bruner (Babin and Harrison). This conference gave rise to the concept of focusing on the processes of writing more than the product. Then in 1966, about fifty teachers of English, primarily from England and the United States, met at Dartmouth College to discuss common problems in the teaching of writing. What the teachers from the US discovered was that in the UK, the teaching of writing was less concerned with writing about literature than promoting students' development through language, believing that the cognitive processes involved in writing were more important than the written products that resulted from the work (Britton, et al.). The trend that began with Alexander Bain to connect writing with psychology is maintained with composition's move away from teaching writing as the teaching of writing about literature. A series of research studies explored what it is writers *do* when they write. For the most part, composition studies remained disconnected from rhetoric and tied to scientific methods. I say "for the most part" because there was one dominant trend, the growth of methods of invention, that integrated rhetorical concepts into the teaching of writing—at least for a time.

All kinds of research was taking place on what writers do, and that took shape as "the writing process" (e.g., Flower and Hayes). The writing process says we begin with random ideas that then take shape in the act of writing, after which we revise what's written, edit, and then make the writing public—meaning for students, turning the paper in. This isn't a linear process; it's recursive. That is, we go back to rethink and revise even during the process of constructing a first draft; we edit as we go along; and we loop through the entire process until we're ready to submit the paper. In the very process of writing, we discover some of what's going on in our minds. The act of writing brings order to what's jumbled in the mind. If you've ever noticed how your writing seems just to take off at a certain point (once you get over the anxiety of having to write or once a deadline forces you to keep writing—the "I write best under pressure" idea), that's what's seen as writing as a means of learning, specifically of learning what's going on in your mind. As a teaching mechanism, "the writing process" has been helpful. But there remains a problem: the mind. Can we really know what the mind is doing since our source for studying the mind *is* the mind?

Composition studies then moves away from trying to come up with universal answers to what happens cognitively when we write (Breuch). The "process" remains helpful as a teaching tool but less so as an explanation. So composition moves toward social construction theory, derived mainly from anthropology and anthropology's research method called ethnographic research. Ethnography is still empirical, still scientific, but it begins to look at patterns that can be tied to cultures, recognizing that the search for universal answers to what folks do in writing can't happen, that there are no truths that can be free from contexts. Everything contains reflections to some extent of the cultural, historical, and political contexts in which inquiry takes place. And to the extent that they are political, they also include points of contact, places where cultures collide, matters I'll get to shortly. But let's return to the rhetoric in "rhetoric and composition" or rhetoric for or within composition.

## The Return to Rhetoric

An explicit connection between composition and rhetoric did not take shape until Edward P. J. Corbett's *Classical Rhetoric for the Modern Student* in 1965. With Corbett's textbook on writing, there is a return to Aristotle and Cicero. More precisely, Corbett adopts a neo-Aristotelian approach to writing, with explicit references to the rhetorical triangle of ethos, pathos, and logos, with *logos* being defined in accordance with a detailed description of Aristotle's systems of logic. Since the textbook provides a wonderful introduction to Classical rhetoric, mainly Aristotle and Cicero, while tied to the teaching of writing, it remains in use today. At about the same time (1968) another rhetorician, Richard Larson, makes the case for returning to Aristotle and Cicero for greater precision in prewriting. The term in rhetoric is *invention.* Although there were specific methods of invention for the various major players in Classical rhetoric—the sophists, Aristotle, Cicero—the overarching method of invention among the Greco-Latin rhetorics was comprised of stasis theory (Crowley). Stasis theory would have a speaker or writer ask four kinds of questions as a means of analysis prior to the speech or paper (in other words, a prewriting exercise). The four kinds of questions would be matters of:

- Conjecture: The fact of the case or argument
- Definition: The meaning/nature of the issue
- Quality: The seriousness of the issue
- Policy: A plan of action

Before writing a paper, writers might ask:

- Conjecture: Were the sources for my paper reliable sources, especially if gathered from the Internet? What makes the sources reliable?

- Definition: What exactly is the issue? And how have my sources brought me to defining the issue?
- Quality: Whom does the issue serve? Or whom could it hurt?
- Policy: Now what? What do we do about the issue?

I emphasize stasis theory because in some sense or other, students are still being asked to approach problems for discussion in assignments with these kinds of questions.

That said, even though rhetoric went through changes over the centuries, not only was composition studies changing in the 1960s, so was rhetoric, in ways that initially influenced forms of invention or prewriting. But as I will argue, the changes in rhetoric have affected current changes in composition studies (apart from the ways in which technology is affecting how we think of writing and the sources of writing). As new ways of approaching rhetoric came into being, so did forms of invention. For instance, following a form of linguistics termed *tagmemic* linguistics, students were asked to create a matrix in defining a situation following the basics of problem solving in quantum mechanics (in that the rhetoric attached to tagmemics came into being at MIT, the Massachusetts Institute of Technology). As a form of invention, the students were asked to describe the problem to be addressed in a paper as a particle, a wave, and a field. To simplify, students would ask:

- Particle: What is the issue to be analyzed exactly?
- Wave: How does the issue change over time?
- Field: What is the issue in a greater context? (Young, Becker, and Pike)

But Kenneth Burke developed what was perhaps the most significant change in rhetoric. In terms of invention, Burke created the dramatistic pentad (*Grammar*). At its core are two older sources. In greater philosophical terms, Burke took a passage from Shakespeare's *As You Like It* quite literally. The character Jaques says that "All the world's a stage, / And all the men and women merely players" (Act II, Scene VII, Lines 138-39). Burke wrote that we can come to some understanding of all human behavior through a method of analysis that relies on the parts of a drama. Those parts are derived from a method that was created by Aristotle to discuss ethics but was developed further for rhetoric by a writer who was believed to be St. Augustine. The questions in Latin were *quis, quid, quando, ubi, cur, quem ad modum, quibus adminiculis* (Robertson). That translates to what students learn as the journalistic 5Ws+H: who, what, when, where, why, and how (with "in what way" or "by what means" being simplified to *how*). Burke converts them to a play, to the stage:

1. Act
2. Scene
3. Agent
4. Agency (or method or means)
5. Purpose (or motive)

But unlike the 5Ws+H, Burke would have us set up the five parts of the pentad as sets of ratios or relationships. To that end, students would be asked to look at the relations from:

- Actor to act
- Actor to scene
- Actor to agency
- Actor to purpose
- Act to scene
- Act to agency
- Act to purpose
- Scene to agency
- Scene to purpose
- Agency to purpose

This was cumbersome—and questionable as a form of prewriting. So in the end, most of these forms of invention sparked by attaching rhetoric to composition would seem to fall away, and what remained was the method of prewriting first discussed by Peter Elbow in his 1973 *Writing without Teachers*.

Elbow called that method freewriting.

We have all done it: just write for a certain amount of time without worrying about editing or rhetorical choices. Just write. What remains of rhetoric that is visible in the composition classroom is the term *kairos*, a Greek word that means "opportunity," but it tends to be used to say something about context and audience (Poulakos).

The terms from Classical rhetoric that continue to be taught in composition seem to remain with ethos, pathos, logos, and now kairos. Yet rhetoric has combined with composition's philosophical connection to social construction in greater, very important ways. To see the connections, however, I'll have to explain a bit of twentieth-century rhetoric.

## The New Rhetoric

The modern age had become (and remains) the age of science. But that science, for all its wonders, also produced weapons of mass destruction, weapons that were used for the obliteration of a people, most of whom were not military. In two days (August 6 and August 9, 1945) over a 100,000 people were killed with just two "bullets," atomic bombs. The aftermath left over a quarter-million dead. That left many wondering how we might tap into our humanity more effectively. One result was the revival of rhetoric, a New Rhetoric. There had been many "new" rhetorics over the centuries (including Alexander Bain's), but most of those new rhetorics weren't truly new at all, and the "new rhetoric" of Bain's time either espoused the rise of literature (what was called *belles lettres*, the beautiful use of writing) or the use of rhetoric for the promotion of science. So something new arose in the mid-twentieth century.

For those of us who study rhetoric, the new rhetoric is seen in terms of a few scholars: the literary critic I. A. Richards; the conservative teacher of composition and more generally English Richard Weaver; the classicist Richard McKeon; the Belgian philosopher Chaïm Perelman with Lucie Olbrechts-Tyteca; and the literary critic (among other things) Kenneth Burke (Gaonkar). Although each of these scholars made significant contributions, the greatest impact on contemporary rhetoric would come from Kenneth Burke. In how Burke defines rhetoric, a door is opened that allows for more recent trends in rhetoric and in composition studies.

The ancient and still most common definition of rhetoric is "the art of persuasion." Although Burke elaborates on that quite a bit, he argues that more important than persuasion is identification. That is, if there is any chance at persuading someone or a group of people, the two sides of the argument have to have some points of agreement, some things in common, things with which they can identify. He also says that where there is identification there is also division. That is, if two people, say, agree on some issue quite completely, there is no need for a rhetorical engagement. There's nothing to persuade. They agree. If two people agree on nothing—literally nothing, not even basic assumptions such that there is complete division—then rhetoric is impossible. If we agree on nothing, there is no common ground from which to work toward persuasion. The realm of rhetoric is in the overlaps of identification and division (see Figure 2.1). The work of rhetoric takes place in the intersection of identification and division, where there is some agreement, some disagreement, and the opportunity, thereby, for some change in one or both parties. In composition studies, we have our differences reflected in different approaches to teaching writing. But we agree on the importance of literacy and of teaching writing. We stand on that base.

The most significant contribution from Burke is his definition of rhetoric:

> *For rhetoric is not rooted in any past condition of human society. It is rooted in an essential function of language itself, a function that is wholly realistic, and is continually born anew; the use of language as a symbolic means of inducing cooperation in beings that by nature respond to symbols.* (Burke, *A Rhetoric* 43)

The first sentence in that definition challenges the official history of rhetoric as something born out of a kind of democracy that

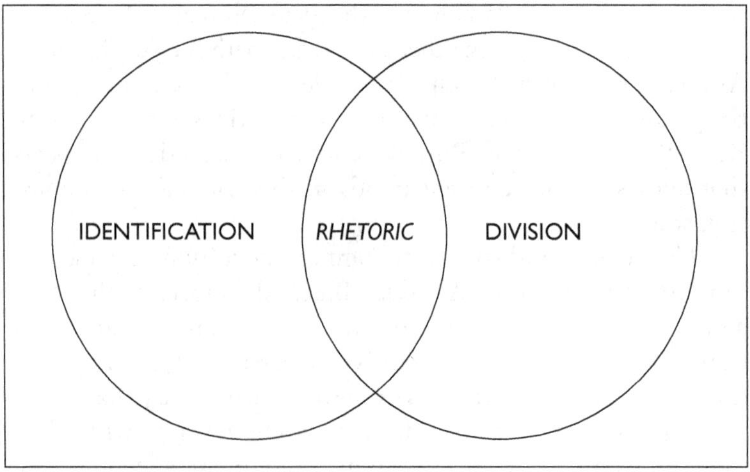


FIGURE 2.1. *The intersection of identification and division.*

took place in the city-state of Athens. I say "a kind of democracy" because women, slaves, and those not born in Athens were not allowed to take part in the governing of the city-state. The creation of democracy, we're told, gave rise to learning how to speak before audiences in making the case for the running of Athens as well as other matters. But Burke writes that where there is language—and anywhere there has been language—there are the roots of rhetoric. And why is that? Because to accomplish anything—fire, cooking, technology, science, and so on—we had to convince one another to cooperate in the making of whatever it was. We did that by using sounds (and later, pictures to represent those sounds, as in the alphabet or any other written form) to represent ideas and things. In other words, language is symbolic. A symbol is something that stands for, or represents, something else. Language is a symbol system, one that is always in motion, always changing or having new things added. Look up the word *meme*, for example. It came from the Greek word for imitation. It then became something that simply gets passed on from one to another (usually by way of imitation) to what is now commonly a reference to something funny passed on through the Internet.

We are creatures who create symbols and who respond to symbols—symbols like clothes to represent skin and hair and fat, or like houses to represent the trees and caves of earliest humans, or even like airplanes to represent the behavior of birds. And in order to create these symbols, we begin with the symbols for things and ideas: words. In a poem Burke titled "Definition of Man" (when *man* still meant all humans, not just male humans), he writes that "Man is the symbol-using (symbol-making, symbol-misusing) animal . . . separated from his natural condition by instruments of his own making" (Burke, *Language* 16). In other words, the thing that makes us unique is not that we have language. We know other creatures have language (for example, dolphins). But no other creature has used language to cooperate in order to transcend so much of nature. There are no dolphin cities, no dolphin planes, no dolphin bombs—that is, symbol using and symbol misusing.

In philosophical terms, Kenneth Burke's definition suggests that our use of language might be ontological. In other words, through our use of language, we would make meaning of the world we're in. I'm not saying we "make" the world; what's real is real. A rock would be there whether we acknowledged it or not. But what that reality *is* to us is made through the language we give to it. A table is a table. But in Spanish, *table* is meaningless; *table* doesn't tell us about a board on legs used for all kinds of social functions. The Spanish speaker would know what it is and its function, but not as *table*. The Spanish speaker would know it as *una mesa*. No doubt this question of language and language use, rhetoric as ontological, is tricky stuff, matters that philosophers have discussed for a few decades. What's more, we really can't know whether Burke intended to suggest that rhetoric is ontological or not, but he surely suggests that rhetoric is epistemological, that how we acquire knowledge requires language and requires our creating ideas and passing on ideas not just through language but through the use of language as a means of cooperation—as rhetoric. Others have come to similar concepts (French philosopher Michele Foucault, for example, though he prefers the word *discourse*).

The term for this connection between rhetoric and epistemology came by way of Robert Scott, a scholar in the discipline of communication: *epistemic* (Harpine). Within composition studies, James Berlin argued that what should happen in a writing classroom is discussions and assignments founded on what he termed an *epistemic rhetoric*; that is, we should discuss where we are and then think and write our ways into how to make a better place, to create a more meaningful life. And this would take place with all students, so we are all of us involved in the betterment of democracy. Meanwhile, the implications of Burke's conception of rhetoric as basic to the being and tied to commonalities (identification) and differences (division) is such that whole new areas of rhetoric have arisen, sometimes with explicit references to Burke and other times not.

## Contrastive Rhetoric

An applied linguist, Robert B. Kaplan, made the case that different cultures have different ways of making arguments. Rather than discuss languages, he discussed the ways different cultures arranged arguments, reflecting their cultural ways even when using different languages. He ran into problems among linguists and others because he overgeneralized: he had all Asians using one kind of rhetoric, for example, when there are so many different Asian languages and cultures. But the concept does make sense. It made sense to me because I had firsthand experience with the matter. Just by chance, I discovered that the problems I had with my own writing in college were tied to the rhetoric of the cultures that were my first until I attended school. Spanish and accented English were what I heard at home, mixed with African American Language. My language ways were what is now called New York Latino English (Slomanson and Newman). My writing favored the first person (like I'm doing here), was highly metaphorical and repetitive, and included tangents I didn't recognize as tangents. In a conference presentation, Kaplan described his research on Puerto Ricans from New York (like me), finding that even when the Puerto Ricans believed themselves to be monolingual in English, they nevertheless displayed the rhetorical patterns of bilingual and Spanish-dominant writers.

Later, as a young rhetorician, I traced the pattern of American Latines (La-teen-es; a matter I'll explain) to the Arab empire, which had conquered Spain in 711 CE and remained in the Iberian

Peninsula until Queen Isabela and King Fernando won the war against the Arab Moors in 1492. A seven-hundred-year-old occupation of the Iberian Peninsula meant some Arab ways had to influence the Spanish of Spain, a Spanish that would then come to the Western Hemisphere with Columbus—in 1492. In terms of Classical rhetoric, the rhetoric of the Spaniards at the time of the conquest of the "New World" would have been Sophistic—ethos-centered, florid, and not necessarily tied to Aristotle's very precise logic (Villanueva). In the Western Hemisphere, contrastive rhetoric would be particularly interesting in contemporary times, given the mixes of cultures from the world as well as the various indigenous people of the hemisphere. Rhetorician LuMing Mao, for example, writes that Chinese American rhetoric is given to indirection: "subtle, direct strategies, through innuendoes and allusions" (61). Test yourself: if your writing teacher questions your logic, maybe you really are having problems making logical connections, or maybe your logic has a different pattern to it. You might be operating out of another rhetoric, a rhetoric that reflects your ancestry. Maybe.

Mentioning the indigenous people of the Western Hemisphere, however, raises an issue in how I approached contrastive rhetoric those many years ago: I didn't account for the rhetoric that would have already been here in the Western Hemisphere when the Spaniards arrived. I remained tied to the idea that rhetoric began in Athens. But the peoples of this hemisphere would have had their own cultures, their own religions. They had even cooperated in building pyramids (more pyramids than the Egyptians, in fact), with the remains of pyramids found in the US (mainly along the Mississippi River), in Mexico, Guatemala, Peru, and more. What Burke's definition of rhetoric tells us is that rhetoric is a part of the human species, that we are rhetorical creatures, that how we come to learn—maybe even how we come to know how to think about reality—is tied to rhetoric. So rhetoric would not have had a single site of origin. Wherever people cooperated through the use of language, their use of language would be their rhetoric. Cultures would have culturally determined rhetorics.

Accordingly, a decidedly new area of rhetoric emerged: comparative rhetoric. The first to coin the phrase was a classicist named George Kennedy (*Comparative*). As a classicist, however, his definition of rhetoric was deeply rooted in the Greco-Roman history of rhetoric. And as a classicist, he appeared disconnected from the New Rhetoric. Kennedy's comparative rhetoric began by arguing that animal societies have rhetorics. And in a strangely Darwinian move, Kennedy went on to look at the rhetorics of Australian aborigines, stating that their rhetoric would be closer to the rhetorics of the nonhuman animals. This is particularly troublesome, given its racist implications. So whereas Kennedy coined an important term, *comparative rhetoric*, he set about proving the universality of the Greco-Roman and the ethnocentric belief in superior beings, at least rhetorically, even among humans. Although the term was new, it reflected the prior understanding of alternative rhetorics. The problem with that term is that there remains a singular "true" rhetoric with all others simply alternatives to that one true rhetoric. Comparative rhetorics—comparisons from the Greco-Roman and others as well as comparisons among the others—remains the most useful term in recognizing there would be no single origin of rhetoric, however, as long as we are willing to walk away from the canonical origin story.

## Women and Rhetoric

Although *comparative rhetoric* is a useful term, its emphasis has been limited to differences among national cultures, not differences related to gender. It might well have been the case that women were excluded from the political workings of the Greco-Roman worlds and much of the rest of Europe and beyond, but surely women spoke, cooperated, identified, and wrote. Perhaps the most noteworthy woman mentioned as part of the world of Athenian Classical rhetoric is Aspasia. She was said to have taken part in conversations with Socrates and other philosophers and rhetoricians of Athens. Rhetorician Cheryl Glenn has even suggested that Aspasia was the teacher of her partner or spouse, the Athenian general and statesman Pericles. Although women of Athens and throughout much of rhetoric's history were not granted the title of rhetorician, they existed and are now beginning to be recognized (Flynn; Lunsford).

Elizabeth Flynn, whose scholarship recovers texts by notable women rhetoricians throughout history, also contributes to the rhetorical differences found in women's writing in first-year composition classes. In "Composing as a Woman," Flynn describes women writers in her class as providing narratives that tell "of interaction, of connection, or frustrated connection." The men, on the other hand, composed stories "of achievement, of separation, or of frustrated achievement" (428). Even though Flynn provided a sample of only four students, she nevertheless began the exploration of what feminist theory and rhetoric could tell us about writing in college classrooms devoted to composition studies.

## African American Language and African American Rhetoric

Within a US framework, there are several works that look not only to women's rhetorics but to the rhetorics of women of color. Shirley Wilson Logan, for example, looks to *The Persuasive Discourse of Nineteenth-Century Black Women* (which is the subtitle to her book, *We Are Coming*). What she describes are Black women of the later nineteenth century who spoke of "uplift" to members of Black women's clubs, where women were concerned with changing the laws so that Black men as well as women would be allowed to vote.

The term *uplift* is an interesting one in terms of nineteenth-century and early twentieth-century African American rhetorics (Orey). The term presupposed an elite cadre of Black women and men whose purpose was to persuade the Black masses to seek out education and refinement. Booker T. Washington, for example, spoke of Black Americans becoming the best at crafts, at industrial work, and at farming, thereby earning the respect of society as a whole. W. E. B. DuBois, on the other hand, saw uplift not through agrarian and industrial education but through academic education. For DuBois, the rhetoricians of uplift would be comprised of "The Talented Tenth," those who would speak of the right to vote, civil rights, and education, much like the women rhetoricians of the women's clubs and the church of the nineteenth century.

But uplift isn't all there is to a Black American rhetoric. In the nineteenth century, it was the rhetoric of the Black church that was most apparent. It consisted of call-and-response, in which the lines between ethos and pathos were blurred. That is, whereas Greco-Roman rhetoric has a speaker whose task is to gain credibility in order to persuade a receptive audience, in call-and-response the speaker receives vocal and gestural responses from the audience that in turn affects the speaker. In Greco-Roman rhetoric there is an implicit linearity, one direction: someone saying something to someone (ethos-> logos->pathos). In the Black tradition, there is an explicit dialogue: someone saying something to someone saying something back. Although structural racism remained, the twentieth century—especially during the final third of the century—saw greater mobility among African Americans and greater exposure both to and from Black Americans. The rhetorical ways of a greater number of Black Americans gained attention among all speakers. The result was and remains a greater understanding of the linguistic ways of African American Language as a legitimate dialect, often referred to as a language because of its unique history as a pidgin and then a creole form of communication. During the Middle Passage from Africa to the US at the time of the slave trade, the slaves were of different cultures and different languages, intentionally mixed together so they couldn't revolt. But humans create language and create rhetoric, we've been told. So the slaves had to create a new way to communicate, and that new way became mixed with English. This creole was called Black English Vernacular, Black English, African American Vernacular English, African American English (and Ebonics, though Ebonics is not unique to English). But since to say African *American* is to speak of English, there is growing use of the term *African American Language* (AAL)—an English particularly mixed with elements of African languages, likely the creole of West Africa, where there was a need to communicate with the British prior to or at the same time as the American slave trade.

Some qualities of AAL tend to be generally known, especially because of the popularity of hip-hop and other exposure through mass media. Yet there are rhetorics that remain more closely tied to the Black community by what Molefi Kete Asante calls Afrocentricity. Literary critic Henry Louis Gates, Jr. notes that this rhetoric betrays certain tropes or figurative language. The most important of these, Gates writes, is signifying. Signifying is a kind of playful insulting, a word game. And there are others, like storytelling and the use of particular inflections (Say whaaaat?), a reflection of African tonal languages, and of course, call-and-response (even to the movie or TV screen).

In terms of composition studies, once AAL was recognized as a legitimate dialect rather than slang—that is, once it was realized that AAL was not just words or phrases of an in-group but was a formal, rule-governed, and historically formulated use of language—composition studies tried to adjust to the needs of the students. But this has been tricky because helping speakers of AAL succeed meant reinforcing the language of power, a power that has historically denigrated AAL. In oral discourse, the language of power is Standard American English (SAE); in writing, it's Edited American English (EAE). The first tendency was to teach writing EAE or SAE the same way one would teach a foreign language. In 1969, linguist and compositionist James Sledd noted that this was fraught with difficulties, not only politically but also in terms of comparative analysis. That is, there simply wasn't enough known about AAL—or even SAE—to make this work. For instance, linguists didn't know if the dropping of a /t/ or an /r/ in oral AAL transferred to dropping them in written AAL; "that's their book" would be said "tha's they book," but would the AAL speaker write it that way? Bidialectalism as a form of teaching English as a quasi-foreign language was not sustainable.

In 1974, members of the Conference on College Composition and Communication declared that teachers should simply respect the dialects of their students. That declaration was published as a document titled "Students' Right to Their Own Language" (SRTOL). By and large, the principle of SRTOL has been accepted over the last four decades but not the practice, again because of the pragmatics of teachers and professors outside of the English classroom who believe that there is a single "correct" English. The compromise has been to teach code-switching. There is a code for academic and business English and a code for the home community. Be conscious of both, goes the argument. Recognize the legitimacy of both and switch according to the context. In other words, make kairotic decisions. Compositionists Vershawn

Ashanti Young, Rusty Barret, Y'Shanda Young-Rivera, and Kim Bryan Lovejoy have argued, however, that code-switching presumes discrete dialects and suggests one stop using all AAL and switch over to SAE or EAE. That, they argue, is not likely. Rather than code-switching, then, Vershawn Ashanti Young in particular argues for code-meshing—that is, incorporating the artifacts of both dialects. Keith Gilyard and Elaine Richardson, though, drop the concern about the phonetics of AAL, the question of whether students write like they speak (a question that never arises with regard to the British English, who are also nonrhotic, meaning they also don't pronounce a final /r/ in many instances; there's more than language use in worrying about the AAL to EAE connection, apparently). In a relatively large empirical study, Gilyard and Richardson, rather than worrying about pronunciation-to-writing, looked to African American Rhetoric, finding that those who employed AAR wrote successfully. In other words, though Gilyard and Richardson make no reference to contrastive rhetoric, they found the oral phonological/pronunciation factors mattered less than the rhetoric employed, finding that when Afrocentric rhetorics are employed, students are more successful.

## Ethnic Rhetorics

In some sense, racialized rhetorics start and end with Black American rhetoric. Although the labels change, some preferring Black, Black Americans, African Americans, Afro-Americans (and Fields and Fields preferring Afro-Americans for the descendants of American slavery and African Americans for the descendants of more recent immigrants from Africa), there is, when writing of the descendants of American slavery, a collective identity that Black Americans themselves can assume. When it comes to those who come from a Spanish ancestry, for example, including the first conquerors of the "New World," the cultural and racialized differences are significant. Our labels betray the differences such that we enter into troubled waters if we try to assert a single "Latino" rhetoric. Even that assertion—"Latino rhetoric"—is contested. I am from a Puerto Rican ancestry. The Puerto Rican Spanish dialect, and in many cases its English manifestations, are very different from the Spanish of the American Southwest. So Chicano rhetoric doesn't apply to me or to any of the Spanish-heritage people of the Caribbean. Although Mestizo rhetoric hearkens to real Mexican history (connecting as it does to the children of Hernán Cortés and his translator and eventually his concubine, la Malinche or Malintzin or Malintze or Malinalli or Doña Marina), the terms *mestizo* and *mestiza* (more on the gendered endings of all of these terms later) are also often used nonliterally as tropes and figures (Fernandez). *Mestiza* is literal, for instance, in the case of writer Gloria Anzaldúa and is the likely inspiration for the term *Mestiza rhetoric* (Lunsford), but the term is less literal among the women writers of the nineteenth century whom rhetoricians Jessica Enoch and Cristina Devereaux Ramírez write about. But in terms of a blanket description, the Spanish-speaking people of the Western Hemisphere are like all others of this hemisphere: Black, White, Asian, and Middle Eastern, no less than indigenous people and all the racial mixes thereto (Vega and Chávez). *Hispanic* is derived from the Latin *Hispanicus*, the term for the peninsula that was *Hispania* before the birth of the nation-state *España*, Spain. But since Spaniards are not necessarily the biological origin of all Spanish speakers (maybe not even most of them), that term, *Hispanic*, again denies the racial and cultural mixes that all in the Western Hemisphere can claim.

The current term, at least among academics and popular media, is *Latinx*. The *x* is to recognize that Latino and Latina represent only two genders and that the terms give rise to a heteronormativity (meaning that one is either a man, Latino, or a woman, Latina, disallowing gay, lesbian, or transgender representation). Despite *Latinx*'s currency, though, there are those who object to the term, insofar as the *x* is an Anglicization. If one is bilingual in English and Spanish, the word can only be said in English—Latin-ex. If one is monolingual in Spanish, like newer immigrants would be, *Latin-ex* would be hard to pronounce (/x/ is pronounced /eh-kees/ in Spanish). *Latin-ex* is English, and that means the word denies those of Spanish-language ancestry (or currency) their linguistic heritage—even among those of us who comport ourselves almost exclusively in English. We may be English speakers (even English professors), but our linguistic heritage should nevertheless be respected. The solution for many from Spanish-speaking ancestry is *Latine* (pronounced /la-teen-eh/), insofar as the final *e* in Spanish is already gender neutral. *Un estudiante* is a student, no matter the gender, nongender, transgender, or sexuality.

All this is to say that there can be no universal Latine rhetoric, since there are so many cultures and linguistic variations (for instance, the word *ahorita* means "right now" for Mexicans and means the exact opposite, "later," for Puerto Ricans). But what we do have in common is a colonial history. Whatever the many, many different indigenous cultures and peoples of this hemisphere, Spanish imperialism unites us all—including those of us living in the United States, since the Spaniards were the first settler colonists of the Western Hemisphere.

Rather than a unified Latine rhetoric, then, contemporary attention has turned to a decolonial rhetoric tied to decolonial theory. Within the US, this theory and its rhetoric are tied to Walter Mignolo, an Argentine literary theorist (though he is also associated with cultural anthropology) primarily because he works in an American university and publishes in English as well as in Spanish. But Mignolo credits Peruvian sociologist Aníbal Quijano ("Delinking") for this theory. That said, the study of decolonial theory features a broad range of mainly Latin American and Latine scholars. But because the history of the Western Hemisphere and the Pacific Ocean's islands are so deeply tied to rhetoric, the interest in decolonial rhetorics ranges far and wide. The US indigenous people, for example, reside in "Indian Nations" (e.g., the Navajo Nation), but they're essentially colonies within the US. What's more, the US still "owns" colonies: Puerto Rico, the US Virgin Islands, Guam, the Commonwealth of the Northern Mariana Islands, and American Samoa. The major premise of decolonial theory is that modernism included colonialism and, in terms of a rhetoric, that colonialism included a kind of colonialism of the mind. In the language of Kenneth Burke, *modernism* becomes an Ultimate Term, a term we tend not to question (Burke, *A Rhetoric*).

So the kinds of thinking that give rise to, say, African American rhetoric, Mestize rhetoric, or comparative rhetorics in the larger sense can all fall under the heading of "decolonial rhetorics." The term that has gathered the most attention within a decolonial rhetoric is *delinking*. Rather than represent (or re-present) the knowledge we have acquired, which would necessarily be tied to modernism and thereby to coloniality, decolonial rhetoric asks that we enunciate—that is, give voice to difference in keeping with the second guiding principle for English studies proposed in the introduction to this collection. This move to "seek difference" makes for a new kind of identification, wherein division is our accustomed way of perceiving ourselves within the world (or at least within a modern, European sensibility). This does not mean starting from scratch. It means being keenly aware that rhetorics and writings and all that is English studies is part of a system of ongoing, adaptive processes called for among twenty-first-century guiding principles for English studies. It means rethinking our identifications. In effect, the process is one of forming a new, adaptive epistemic. A particular example comes by way of American Indian rhetorics. In rhetorical terms, stories in a conventional, Classical rhetorical way of thinking would be a metonymy. That is, the story is a piece of life, an example that (if done well) tells a much larger tale. But for American Indian rhetoric, the story *is* the rhetoric *and* a literature, a rethinking of what constitutes both. American Indian rhetoric, in line with the third principle of a contemporary principle of English studies, is to be regarded as a literature. There are different epistemologies involved that need to be recognized and acknowledged (Powell). Nor is this particular to American Indian rhetorics. For Kenneth Burke, literature no less than rhetoric is "symbolic action."

## Perhaps to Translingualism as Decolonial Rhetoric

In terms of teaching writing, decolonial rhetoric becomes tied with the critical consciousness articulated by Paulo Freire in 1970 (in English; the original Portuguese version was published two years earlier). Although Freire predates the *decolonial* as a term, his teaching theory's aims remain the same as the decolonial: to question the things we tend not to question, more than problem solving but problem posing, asking us to "embrace the collaborative" (guiding principle number six from the introduction to this collection) as culture circles. Fifty years later, teachers of composition still seek to have students do the deep questioning Freire promotes. To this, we might add rhetorical listening, wherein we recognize that collaboration involves listening to the views of others and the views of the Othered: women, LGBTQ+ communities, people of color, and those from other cultures, all of whose rhetorical ways might be quite different from our everyday discourses, as in the example of hearing the "argument" in a story told by an indigenous person. In composition studies, the move is for a greater understanding of translingualism, the explicit understanding that we are, all of us, given to different languages and different ways with language, from cultural differences to idiolects (our very personal, individual ways with language). Translingualism provides an interesting set of conversations, recognizing that the "traditional classroom" is undergoing a new tradition. The questions then become "How do we recognize our differences?" "How do we delink without becoming victims to the linguistic power we all recognize continues to exist, the power of Standard American English and Edited American English?" The answer might well be to develop a metalinguistic awareness (Hartwell, 1985), becoming conscious of language-as-language and remaining rhetorically conscious—thus, all of us becoming rhetoricians.

## Works Cited

Aristotle. *On Rhetoric: A Theory of Civic Discourse*. Translated by George A. Kennedy, 2nd ed., Oxford UP, 2007.

Asante, Molefi Kete. *Afrocentricity*. Africa World P, 1988.

Babin, Edith, and Kimberly Harrison. "Jerome Bruner." *Contemporary Composition Studies: A Guide to Theorists and Terms*, Greenwood, 1999, p. 272.

Bain, Alexander. *English Composition and Rhetoric: A Manual*. BiblioBazaar, 2016.

Berlin, James A. *Rhetoric and Reality: Writing Instruction in American Colleges, 1900–1985*. Southern Illinois UP, 1987.

Breuch, Lee-Ann M. Kastman. "Post-Process 'Pedagogy': A Philosophical Exercise." *JAC*, vol. 22, no. 1, 2002, pp. 119–50.

Britton, James, Tony Burgess, Nancy Martin, et al. *The Development of Writing Abilities (11–18)*. Macmillan, 1975.

Burke, Kenneth. *A Grammar of Motives*. U California P, 1969.

———. *A Rhetoric of Motives*. U California P, 1969.

———. *Language as Symbolic Action: Essays on Life, Literature, and Method*. U California P, 1966.

Corbett, Edward P. J., and Robert J. Connors. *Classical Rhetoric for the Modern Student*. 4th ed., Oxford UP, 1999.

Crowley, Sharon. *The Methodical Memory: Invention in Current-Traditional Rhetoric*. Southern Illinois UP, 1990.

Elbow, Peter. *Writing Without Teachers*. 2nd ed., Oxford UP, 1998.

Enoch, Jessica, and Cristina Devereaux Ramírez. *Mestiza Rhetorics: An Anthology of Mexicana Activism in the Spanish-Language Press, 1887–1922*. Southern Illinois UP, 2019.

Fernandez, Miriam Lizette. *Tropes of the Nation: Tracing the Colonial Origins of the Matriarchal Figures of Mexican Nationalism*. 2018. Washington State U, PhD dissertation.

Fields, Karen E., and Barbara J. Fields. *Racecraft: The Soul of Inequality in American Life*. Verso, 2012.

Flower, Linda, and John R. Hayes. "A Cognitive Process Theory of Writing." *College Composition and Communication,* vol. 32, no. 4, Dec. 1981, pp. 365–87.

Flynn, Elizabeth A. "Composing 'Composing as a Woman': A Perspective on Research." *College Composition and Communication,* vol. 41, no. 1, Dec. 1990, pp.83–89.

Freire, Paulo. *Pedagogy of the Oppressed*. Translated by Myra Bergman Ramos, Herder and Herder, 1970.

Gaonkar, Dilip Parameshwar. "The Revival of Rhetoric, the New Rhetoric, and the Rhetorical Turn: Some Distinctions." *Informal Logic*, vol. 15, no. 1, winter 1993, pp. 53–64.

Gates, Henry Louis, Jr. "The Signifying Monkey and the Language of Signifyin(g)." *The Rhetorical Tradition: Readings from Classical Times to the Present,* edited by Patricia Bizzell and Bruce Herzberg, Bedford, 1990, pp.1185–223.

Gilyard, Keith, and Elaine Richardson. "Students' Right to Possibility: Basic Writing and African American Rhetoric." *Insurrections: Approaches to Resistance in Composition Studies*, edited by Andrea Greenbaum, State U of New York P, 2001, pp. 37–51.

Glenn, Cheryl. "Sex, Lies, and Manuscript: Refiguring Aspasia in the History of Rhetoric." *College Composition and Communication*, vol. 45, no. 2, May 1994, pp.180–99.

Harned, Jon. "The Intellectual Background of Alexander Bain's 'Modes of Discourse.'" *College Composition and Communication*, vol. 36, no. 1, Feb. 1985, pp. 42–50.

Harpine, William D. "What Do You *Mean*, Rhetoric Is Epistemic?" *Philosophy & Rhetoric*, vol. 37, no. 4, 2004, pp. 335–52.

Hartwell, Patrick. "Grammar, Grammars, and the Teaching of Grammar." *College English*, vol. 47, no. 2, Feb. 1985, pp.105–27.

Kaplan, Robert B. "Cultural Thought Patterns and Intercultural Education." *Language Learning*, vol. 16, no. 1–2, 1966, pp. 1–20.

Kennedy, George A. *Classical Rhetoric and Its Christian and Secular Tradition from Ancient to Modern Times*. U North Carolina P, 1980.

———. *Comparative Rhetoric: An Historical and Cross-Cultural Introduction*. Oxford UP, 1998.

Logan, Shirley Wilson. *We Are Coming: The Persuasive Discourse of Nineteenth-Century Black Women*. Southern Illinois UP, 1999.

Lunsford, Andrea A. "Toward a Mestiza Rhetoric: Gloria Anzaldúa on Composition and Postcoloniality." *JAC*, vol. 18, no. 1, 1998, pp. 1–27.

Mao, LuMing. *Reading Chinese Fortune Cookie: The Making of Chinese American Rhetoric*. Utah State UP, 2006.

Mignolo, Walter D. "Delinking." *Cultural Studies*, vol. 21, no. 2–3, Mar. 2007, pp. 449–514.

Orey, Byron D'Andra. "Explaining Black Conservatives: Racial Uplift or Racial Resentment?" *The Black Scholar*, vol. 34, no. 1, 2004, pp. 18–22.

Plato. *Phaedrus and Letters VII and VIII*. Translated by Walter Hamilton, Penguin, 1973.

Poulakos, John. "Toward a Sophistic Definition of Rhetoric." *Philosophy & Rhetoric*, vol. 16, no. 1, 1983, pp. 35–48.

Powell, Malea. "Stories Take Place: A Performance in One Act." *College Composition and Communication*, vol. 64, no. 2, 2012, pp. 383–406.

Robertson, D. W., Jr. "A Note on the Classical Origin of 'Circumstances' in the Medieval Confessional." *Studies in Philology*, vol. 43, no. 1, Jan. 1946, pp. 6–14.

Sledd, James. "Bi-Dialectalism: The Linguistics of White Supremacy." *The English Journal,* vol. 58, no. 9, Dec. 1969, pp. 1307–29.

Slomanson, Peter, and Michael Newman. "Peer Group Identification and Variation in New York Latino English *laterals*." *English World-Wide*, vol. 25, no. 2, Jan. 2004, pp. 199–216.

Vega, Karrieann Soto, and Karma R. Chávez. "Latinx Rhetoric and Intersectionality in Racial Rhetorical Criticism." *Communication and Critical/Cultural Studies*, vol. 15, no. 4, 2018, pp. 319–25.

Villanueva, Victor. *Bootstraps: From an American Academic of Color.* NCTE, 1993.

Young, Richard E., Alton L. Becker, and Kenneth L. Pike. *Rhetoric: Discovery and Change.* Harcourt, 1970.

Young, Vershawn Ashanti, Rusty Barret, Y'Shanda Young-Rivera, and Kim Brian Lovejoy. *Other People's English: Code-Meshing, Code-Switching, and African American Literacy.* Parlor Press, 2018.

# *Creative Writing*

SARAH E. SANDMAN
*Purdue University Fort Wayne*

*Instructions for living a life.*
*Pay attention.*
*Be astonished.*
*Tell about it.*
—Mary Oliver

What if, instead of beginning with a history of the field for this chapter about creative writing (histories are important for sure, and I'll include a bibliography for you to peruse), I told you I was going to weave stories that show the creative writing world as it is today. Let me be clearer: this world of creative writing is ever changing, dynamic, and specific for each writer who inhabits it. Some writers spend their days traveling to give book talks, some writers work three jobs and write poetry on napkins, some writers self-publish because their stories mean everything to them. *This* creative writing world is populated with people of all genders, ages, sexualities, ethnicities, and skill levels. We mustn't just talk about literary creative writing anymore—we must look to all spaces where imaginative writing is happening.[1]

We must also remember that creative writing doesn't happen in a vacuum—moreover, creative writing as a discipline is found within English studies, where it is in dialogue with linguistics, rhetoric and composition, literature and literary criticism, critical theory and cultural studies, and English education. Perhaps more so than any other discipline in English studies, creative writing represents each of its family members. Students in creative writing programs have taken linguistics to understand language at its roots, learned about the undergirding of rhetoric in communication, studied literature and what the critics say about that literature, and found themselves immersed within critical theory and cultural studies as they read broadly to become better writers. Creative writing is also an important component of English education, as teaching future teachers to write stories helps them someday teach their students. In other words, despite the once narrow-minded publishing industry that was dominated by a white male gaze, the creative writing discipline has continued to gain relevance and importance within the academic spaces of English studies.

Because a career as a creative writer is often nebulous, this chapter uses stories of writers to show how one might craft a career as a creative writer. The chapter will also look to one of the most prolific landscapes of publishing there is today to help show how diverse creative writing is now: the literary magazine.

Stories matter, and so do the people who write them.

It's been two days since Mary Oliver died. When I heard the news, I thought I may have to pull over my car. I immediately sent a text to my colleague Erica who works with me for the literary magazine I started, *The Dandelion Review*. Erica is a great example of a contemporary writer—she has an MFA from Bennington College (a preeminent program for poetry). Her poetry is beautiful and fierce, but she doesn't get to write poetry to make a living. This is an unfortunate fact about the creative writing world, a fact I always tell my students about. You are unlikely to make a living as a poet unless you are also working as an academic. Then, perhaps you could consider that your work, to teach poetry, is also part of your work of being a writer. Nevertheless, Erica carves out ways to interact with the poetry world. She hosts readings and events in our city, she works as social media director for *The Dandelion Review,* and she continues to write poems and send out her writing. She is a published poet, many times over, and she is a good example of a person who is an important part of the web of creative writing.

When Erica received the text from me telling her about Mary Oliver, she was grief-stricken, and then responded, "we must plan something." *The Dandelion* should host an event. And so it went—we had an event where we invited writers and musicians to pay tribute to Mary Oliver, to her work and what she has done for us. Maybe thinking about the reading is why I feel so compelled to say that poetry *matters*. Maybe it's because so many of my friends and colleagues have posted on social media their favorite Oliver poems with tender stories about how her writing saved them, sometimes literally. But here I am, paying attention, as Mary Oliver taught me to do.

It makes sense to open a chapter about creative writing by mentioning one of the most influential poets of the twentieth century—and maybe even the twenty-first century. While this chapter isn't just about poetry, neither was Mary Oliver just a poet. She was a writer who captured daily living in the most nuanced and beautiful ways. She said, "Tell me, what is it you plan to do / with your one wild and precious life?" ("The Summer Day").

## Endless Possibilities

I'll start with myself. Hi, you can call me Sarah.

In truth, that's how I introduce myself each semester to my students. I teach at a midwestern university where my course load consists of introductory creative writing classes about poetry, fiction, and creative nonfiction.

I'll often tell my students how I got to be the person who gets to teach them. I came to the creative writing world from passion and instinct, a drive to write poetry that came out of me like breath. I didn't take a traditional path, though. I have an undergraduate degree in English with a concentration in writing. I have a master's degree in English with a concentration in writing and American literature. My story is unlike some in that I don't have an MFA (master of fine arts, what has generally been known as the terminal degree for a creative writer). A good friend of mine, Curtis Crisler, a brilliant poet, went from his undergraduate program to an MFA program, and he teaches with me at my university. When I finished my master's degree, I had to make a choice. Should I try to get an MFA and make it as a poet, or should I take a more secure route and get a PhD, knowing I would likely be able to get a job teaching composition? In this case, because of my life circumstances at the time, it is true that I took the practical route. I have a PhD in composition and rhetoric—and that means I'm qualified to teach all kinds of writing. In addition to studying composition and rhetoric, I was lucky enough to be in a PhD program that allowed me to take creative writing workshops as well. My story is perhaps nontraditional in that I have been able to carve out a path where I get to teach and study many kinds of writing, including creative writing. My PhD program at Ball State University was filled with opportunities to study with important writers like Jill Christman, Mark Neeley, and Sean Lovelace. The Ball State staff has expanded greatly since I've been there. Their master's degree with a creative writing concentration offers students the opportunity to hone their skills in a multigenre program while studying with well-published faculty. Then, students can choose which path they go down next—perhaps an MFA or a PhD in creative writing or entering into some kind of professional writing career.

When I was hired for the job I have now, I was to teach professional writing courses like business writing and composition courses like the typical English 101. This was fine by me because having a job was the most important part. As I settled into my job, though, there was an opportunity for me to teach the introductory creative writing class. I leapt at this chance, and the rest is history, as they say.

But that part of my story is just the academic one—what about how I live in the creative writing industry?

Not only am I a teacher, but I am also a writer who writes poetry and creative nonfiction, a literary magazine editor, and a writing coach. My academic training and my teaching career prepared me to be able to find my way into more creative writing outlets.

Here are two more stories of creative writers in today's industry. Bethanne is a freelance writer whose income comes from being a journalist. She writes book reviews for the *Washington Post, Time* magazine, and other major media outlets. For years, she has been an integral part of the book critics circle. She also is a memoirist. For Bethanne, it has been really important to find a way to sell her memoir. She works with an agent, and she wrote a proposal with a sample chapter. Her book was purchased by Counterpoint Press. Bethanne's situation is not necessarily the normal one—not many writers get their books purchased from a proposal. However, it certainly can happen!

Counterpoint Press is a great example of where much of the publishing industry is headed. While publishing is still ruled by the Big 5 (or 6)—Macmillan, Hachette, HarperCollins, Penguin Books, Random House, and Simon & Schuster—it is places like Counterpoint that disrupt the cost-analysis-driven publishing industry. Counterpoint says this about themselves:

> Author-driven, we devote all energy to the fresh, cutting-edge, and literary voices of our authors. The genres we cover are vast—fiction and nonfiction, poetry, graphic novels, and anthologies, all of which collectively focus on current affairs and politics, counterculture, music, history, memoir, literary biography, religion, and philosophy. (counterpointpress.com)

What we have been seeing in the industry is a move toward smaller presses, independent presses, and presses that are willing to allow for author input.

One final story is about Dori. Dori is a children's librarian with a bachelor's degree in English and a concentration in British literature. Dori always had a dream of writing for children, and she took the step to get an MFAC. (An MFAC is a master's degree in writing for children.) Hamline University is one of the best programs in the nation for obtaining an MFAC, and Dori chose the program for many reasons. Some may say: I don't need a degree to write. This, of course, is true. However, getting an MFA(C) isn't only about becoming a better writer. These programs are rigorous in their reading requirements and in the amount of writing each student produces. The programs ask students to find their boundaries and push past them, reaching writing spaces they didn't believe they had. And these programs are about creating connections, networking, and community building. The myth of writers spending their days in a faraway room, writing by themselves, is just that: a myth. Writing is actually a communal practice that involves many other readers.

The program at Hamline is a low-residency program. Low residency means that students write and read from wherever they are and work in correspondence with a professor. This kind of program is perfect for students who don't wish to do traditional coursework and who would like to spend most of their time writing. Students are paired with a professor each semester, and they work closely together. One or two times a year, students go to the campus of the school and are "in residence." The residencies are comprised of lectures, workshopping each other's writing, faculty and student readings, etc.

There are many opportunities for writers to create networks, perhaps as many as there are unique writers. There isn't a right or a wrong way to find one's path into the creative writing world. The best way in is the way that feels the most comfortable for the writer and that supports whatever the writer's goals are for their present life.

## Literary Magazines: Where So Much Publishing Happens

Literary magazines are an integral part of the field of creative writing. We might think of them as the workhorses of the industry because they publish so much writing every year. This chapter is an attempt to not only show you stories of actual people working in the creative writing world but also to showcase one of the main sources of publishing. Chances are, you'll encounter literary magazines as either a writer submitting your work, as a person working on staff, or maybe even as a publisher running your own.

A literary magazine is a publication that specializes in creative writing by many writers (one genre or multiple genres). For example, a magazine (labeled this because they used to exclusively be in print and be published on some kind of rotating schedule: monthly, quarterly, biannually, annually), might specialize in fiction, or it might include two or three major genres. It could only publish flash fiction like *Flash Fiction Magazine* or very short creative nonfiction like *Brevity*. The more literary magazines that have come into the market, the more specialized they are. Magazines have often been linked to universities, but increasingly they exist as standalone entities.

When the literary magazine *Poetry* was started in 1912 by Harriet Monroe, it was a place for professional writers to publish. As the rise of academic jobs has included creative writing, so too has the importance of literary magazines become part of academic culture. Many academics are required to publish for their promotion cases. Because of this element, they look to publish in all kinds of places, including literary magazines. *Poetry*, for example, has become one of the most renowned places for poets to place their work.

The history of literary magazines is deep and rich. *The North American Review*, founded in 1815, is the oldest literary magazine in the United States. Other well-known literary magazines include *The New Yorker* (started in 1925), *Ploughshares*, (started in 1971, a university, noncommercial magazine), *Paris Review* (started in 1953), and *Tin House* (started in 1998 and one of the most awarded literary magazines). Other important online magazines include *Pank*, *Rattle*, and *The Rumpus*.

Literary magazines serve many populations of writers, not just academics needing to publish for their promotion. Magazines are spaces for writers to get their work in the world without the long process of publishing a book. Being published in notable magazines provides exposure for writers trying to make a name for themselves. Magazines also serve a purpose for the inherent need of a writer: to be heard. Literary magazines provide audiences with the most up-to-date publishing especially because in some forms they publish online and even daily. Finally, when magazines are run by a university, they bring a good reputation to departments. Many students want to work in the editing world, and being able to work on the staff of a literary magazine is great editing experience.

## How Do Literary Magazines Work?

Because there are so many spaces to publish, literary magazines will often solicit work from certain populations of writers. For example, a magazine may only publish work by women or by writers of color. Once a magazine has decided which genre(s) they want to focus on, they will put out a call. Calls give important information about submission details—and writers can find calls in places like *Poets & Writers* magazine. Submissions are gathered, usually from some kind of platform like Submittable, where writers submit their work for what is called a "blind" review. Editors and staff read submissions without any identifying material. Once the editorial staff has made decisions about who will be published, then writers are given a response about their inclusion in the publication. Some publications ask that writers only submit to them; others allow for simultaneous submission. Depending on how fast the magazine produces its issue, writers could see their work up within a week or a month but sometimes not for a year. (Large magazines have big backlogs of accepted work.) As a writer, it's very important to choose a literary magazine that resonates with your focus and style. It is always a good choice to narrow the field of possible magazines to submit to by finding the ones that best mirror your work. Take a look at what a magazine has been publishing—see if the writing sounds like you. When you find the magazine(s) that seems like a good fit, follow the submission guidelines the magazine has posted.

Most literary magazines aren't able to pay writers, though they may compensate them with issues of the magazine in which they appear. Sometimes larger magazines are able to pay a small stipend to a writer. In other words, writers are submitting to literary magazines because publications get their work in the world, not because they are making much money. There are exceptions, however: It is common practice for science fiction magazines to pay by the word for selected stories, for example.

So if running a magazine doesn't provide any financial gain, and if submitting to a magazine doesn't provide a financial gain, why does anyone want to do it? Stephanie Burt wonders, too:

> Why on Earth would you start a literary magazine? You won't get rich, or even very famous. You'll have to keep your day job, unless you're a student or so rich you don't need a day job. You and your lucky friends and the people you hire—if you can afford to pay them—will use their time and energy on page layouts, bookkeeping, distribution, Web site coding and digital upkeep, and public readings and parties and Kickstarters and ways to wheedle big donors or grant applications so that you can put out issue two, and then three. You'll lose time you

could devote to your own essays or fiction or poems. Once your journal exists, it will wing its way into a world already full of journals, like a paper airplane into a recycling bin, or onto a Web already crowded with literary sites. Why would you do such a thing? ("The Persistence of Litmags")

## *The Dandelion Review*

A number of years ago, a colleague and I wanted to start a national literary magazine at our campus. We believed the magazine would bring good exposure to our English department, and it would allow us to teach our students the ins and outs of editing with a practical application. For a number of reasons, mostly financial, the magazine wasn't able to get off the ground. I was saddened that we wouldn't be able to provide a space for up-and-coming writers. I was also in the process of sending out essays—memoir pieces that included discussions of my past abuse and included stories of my now-wife. Editor after editor turned down my work but with a caveat: *your work is beautiful and lyrical, but it just isn't a good fit for us*. This sentiment played over and over in my head. Beautiful and lyrical, but not right for us. Why wasn't my work right? Where would it fit if not in these carefully chosen places?

It was after getting rejected so many times, but knowing it wasn't because of the quality of my work, that I decided I certainly wasn't the only one experiencing this. That's when I decided to start my own literary magazine—which has now also turned into a small chapbook press as well. I wanted to solicit submissions from a specific group of writers with a specific perspective: at first the magazine was for women and gender-nonconforming people. Here's what the website says:

> *The Dandelion Review* earns its name from the hardy flower that so often colors Midwest grasses and that so often burrows up through cracks in the cement. We love these beauties—we're maybe obsessed.
>
> *The Dandelion Review* is a literary magazine publishing poetry and creative nonfiction. We seek to publish women writers and people who identify on the lgbtqiaa+ spectrum.

> We are interested in the stories you have to tell—the quiet morning with your lover, the spilled milk on the floor, the trauma, the survival, the muddy river near your house. We also seek the stories that you *need* to tell. The ones you must write, and the ones you think no one wants to hear. We want to hear them. We really do.
>
> Tell us with leaping language and tight line breaks, with images we've never known, with a shape-shifting essay.

You'll notice that the submissions are now open to women and anyone on the lgtbqiaa+ spectrum. Additionally, I am very interested in all the stories other magazines don't feel comfortable publishing. In my first issue of the magazine, not only were there trauma stories, but there were many stories of women taking care of children, of spouses, of their aging parents. These care stories are often gritty and yet so important for our cultural consciousness. As the rise of memoir, the personal essay, and LGBTQ advocacy continues, our field must also rise up and provide spaces for the stories that come in the personal essay and from writers who identify on the LGBTQ spectrum.

Here's how the magazine happens and how many magazines function.

Writers submit their work in a Word file or a pdf to *The Dandelion Review*'s email address. (If I were a larger magazine, I would likely use a submission platform like Submittable.) After the reading period closes, reviewers read through each submission and sort them into *yes* and *no* files. As the head editor, I'll make the final decision on all pieces.

Acceptances are sent out with a boilerplate that says: "*The Dandelion Review* will have First Electronic Rights to publish my piece/s, as well as First Serial Rights to publish my piece/s in hard copy/print. Otherwise, I will retain all rights to my work. I understand that snippets of my work may be used to promote *The Dandelion Review* via social media, but that in every instance I will be given full credit for my work and (where possible), *The Dandelion Review* will link to my personal internet presence in order to promote me as the author of the piece/s." A boilerplate like this is important because it protects the magazine and it protects the writer.

Writers then respond regarding whether or not they want to move forward with publication. Next, pieces are put in order based on content and language. I merge the documents into a 6" × 9" template, and multiple stages of copyediting happen.

In an era when magazines don't make much money, if any at all, digital spaces and on-demand publishers are often used. I use lulu.com, which is an on-demand publisher. This means that I can order as many copies of the magazine as I want without having to preorder a certain number. This also means that I can use lulu.com as the storing house for the magazine. Anyone who wants to purchase the magazine can do so through the website.

## What's Left?

Creative writing has been a central component of English studies, and creative writing continually serves as a way of envisioning an antidote to "zombified discourses" (see the introduction for more on zombified discourses). Editors of creative writing publications are in an important historical moment that allows for a negotiation of who is welcomed. It is up to magazine editors and small-press editors, especially, to forge the way in the continued attempt to expand what counts as literature. While this expansion of membership also happens in the classroom through awakened professors and updated curricula that incorporate many modes and genres of production to model creative writing and that make space for many kinds of voices, this negotiation begins with our collective attempt to break down racist, sexist, and homophobic institutions.

Further, English studies has always been categorized by its adherence to the importance of reading and writing. Sometimes revolutionary acts happen by simple practices—and so I argue in this conclusion that one of the most revolutionary acts a person can do is to seek difference in the creative writing they choose to read. Seeking difference in reading matters and will lead to more advocating for writers of color, for women writers, and for writers on the LGBTQ spectrum.

To end, a few more lines from Mary Oliver: "Poetry is a life-cherishing force. For poems are not words, after all, but fires for the cold, ropes let down to the lost, something as necessary as bread in the pockets of the hungry. Yes indeed." Here's to finding your "fires for the cold" and your "something as necessary as bread." And here's to looking forward to seeing your work in print.

*Yes, indeed.*

## Note

1. Here I'm using the phrase "imaginative writing" as Janet Burroway uses it—the idea that all writing is imaginative.

## Selected Bibliography


Adsit, Janelle, editor. *Critical Creative Writing: Essential Readings on the Writer's Craft*. Bloomsbury Academic, 2018.

Alison, Jane. *Meander, Spiral, Explode: Design and Pattern in Narrative*. Catapult, 2019.

*Association of Writers & Writing Programs*. www.awpwriter.org

"Best Books for Writers." *Poets & Writers*. https://www.pw.org/best-books-for-writers

*Brevity: A Journal of Concise Literary Nonfiction*. www.brevitymag.com

Burroway, Janet, et al. *Writing Fiction: A Guide to Narrative Craft*, 9th ed. Pearson, 2014.

———. *Imaginative Writing: The Elements of Craft*. 4th ed., Pearson, 2014.

Burt, Stephanie. "The Persistence of Litmags." *The New Yorker*, 7 July, 2015.

*Creative Nonfiction*. www.creativenonfiction.org

Dillard, Annie. *The Writing Life*. Harper Perennial, 2013.

———. *Living by Fiction*. Harper& Row, 1982.

Galef, David. *Brevity: A Flash Fiction Handbook*. Columbia University Press, 2016.

Gardner, John. *On Becoming a Novelist.* W. W. Norton & Company, 1999.

———. *The Art of Fiction: Notes on Craft for Young Writers.* Vintage, 1991.

Goldberg, Natalie. *Writing Down the Bones: Freeing the Writer Within.* Shambhala, 2016.

Harbach, Chad. *MFA vs NYC: The Two Cultures of American Fiction.* Farrar, Straus and Giroux, 2014.

Hoagland, Tony. *The Art of Voice: Poetic Principles and Practices.* W. W. Norton & Company, 2019.

Hugo, Richard. *The Triggering Town: Lectures and Essays on Poetry and Writing.* W. W. Norton & Company, 2010.

Karr, Mary. *The Art of Memoir.* Harper Perennial, 2016.

King, Stephen. *On Writing: A Memoir of the Craft.* Scribner, 2010.

Lamott, Anne. *Bird by Bird: Some Instructions on Writing and Life.* Anchor, 1995.

Lerner, Betsy. *The Forest for the Trees.* Riverhead Books, 2010.

McGurl, Mark. *The Program Era: Postwar Fiction and the Rise of Creative Writing.* Harvard University Press, 2011.

McQuade, Molly, editor. *By Herself: Women Reclaim Poetry.* Graywolf Press, 2000.

Myers, D. G. *The Elephants Teach: Creative Writing Since 1880.* Prentice Hall, 1996.

*The New Yorker.* www.newyorker.com

Oliver, Mary. *A Poetry Handbook.* Mariner Books, 1994.

*Poets & Writers.* www.pw.org

Stafford, William. *Writing the Australian Crawl: Views on the Writer's Vocation.* University of Michigan Press, 1978.

Warner, John. *The Writer's Practice: Building Confidence in Your Nonfiction Writing.* Penguin Books, 2019.

Wood, James. *How Fiction Works.* Picador, 2009.

Chapter Four

# *Literature and Literary Criticism*

Richard C. Taylor
*East Carolina University*

My own career as a scholar and teacher of literature has, from the start, been deeply informed by the sense of my place within the larger framework of English studies. My doctoral work in the 1980s was, for example, heavily influenced by the emerging specialization in rhetoric and composition, which challenged the all-too-common denigration of pedagogically based scholarship, compelled serious critics of literature to reconsider their approaches to audience and genre, and offered a variety of challenging new theoretical approaches that should have made specialists in the traditional literary fields and rhetoric-composition specialists natural allies rather than disciplinary rivals.

At the same time, the emerging study of technical and professional communication offered valuable frameworks within which to embrace the advent of the digital age, which utterly remade our sense of scholarship and teaching. Many of us also found new developments in the field of linguistics invigorating and relevant in our approaches to grammar, orality, and the structures of communication. Those of us who dared sample creative writing seminars found the intense focus on language and stylistic choice a boon to our own writing and teaching about the written word. All of us within English studies as it was then configured shared a thrilling and expanding sense of what a text could convey, how it might mean.

The other prefatory note I should make before focusing my gaze more specifically on trends in literary study is my own mid-career turn from a specialist in eighteenth-century British literature to postcolonial literature and ethnic studies. The shift happened concurrently with some wrenchingly painful institutional fissures that further widened the gap in what should have been collegial interdisciplinary diversity and productive collaboration. My later career has focused on administering programs in multiethnic literature that have grown dramatically, as offerings in the conventional areas of British and American literature have diminished. In spite of the new banner I've been waving, I nonetheless maintain both a respect and affection for the literatures that first brought me to the profession, even though I acknowledge their limitations. Both of these circumstances—the sense of my work as part of a community of scholar-teachers devoted to the study of texts and their production and my sense of literature as necessarily moving beyond the chauvinistic borders once established for it—have informed my approach to the profession I've enjoyed for more than thirty years.

The prospect of surveying the field of literature and literary criticism is daunting unless one finds a fairly specific narrative thread to suggest one way that meaning and discovery are made by scholars in the discipline(s). My interest concerns what might be categorized as a literature of engagement, one that challenges previous disciplinary schemes and theories and sees communication with the "real world" as an essential element for writers, scholars, and readers in general. Disciplinary processes—formation and organization of new fields of study and their institutionalization—have always been fascinating, particularly in times as revolutionary as these past few decades have been in English studies and, particularly, in the study of literature.

For most practitioners, the discipline is experienced primarily as local: the particular challenges and quarrels facing an individual department may or may not be in sync with larger academic trends. Disciplines need common ground, of course: common language and rhetoric, common sets of theoretical assumptions, common credentialing and evaluative criteria, and so forth. Many departments have operated without consensus and with the most fragile of ties. Many have reconstituted themselves or refocused their priorities.

## Stories of Origin

The cohesiveness of our sense of discipline comes, in part, from the stories we share—implicitly and explicitly—about the origins and arc of our practice. Typically, they privilege the contemporary as a corrective to a flawed past and reassure practitioners that their field is progressive, malleable, moving toward some sort of ideal: in the past, we focused on the history surrounding the production of a literary work or perhaps the author's biography at the expense of the text itself; in the past, we ignored the ideological implications of our choices but have become sensitive to the diversity of our literatures and the consequences of our own prejudices; at one time, we experienced a kind of patriotic mandate for our professional work in establishing a distinctive and nation-building literary historical narrative; once, we studied texts as if they were somehow separable from issues of class, race, and gender, and now we are making enlightened choices that better represent our student-readers and the diversity of our texts. The narrative of progress is self-congratulatory and perpetuates a kind of continuity. Practitioners respect the underlying mission of their forebears: to progress as critics, scholars, readers, and teachers of texts, even if this mission is framed—as it often is—in contradistinction to the generations of scholarship that fell short in some fundamental way and needed to be corrected and replaced.

Broad social changes and developments in English studies over the past several decades have necessitated dramatic changes in our approach to teaching literature. Perhaps the urgency of making these changes goes beyond our faith in professional progress and goes to the very survival of literary study as a valuable and visible part of the university's mission. It is increasingly apparent that the literature packaged for students and the works at the center of our critical discourse must be responsive to the external world. That may seem like an obvious requirement for some, and yet the powerful hold of the "New Criticism" on the profession created resistance to reforming curricula and approaches.

The New Criticism framed itself in narrative terms as a corrective to a kind of simple historicism that led a new generation of scholars in the aftermath of World War II—and their baby boom and G.I. Bill-sponsored students—to turn their classrooms into linguistic laboratories of sorts. There, the *Oxford English Dictionary* served as a kind of microscope and the practice of *explication de texte* was celebrated as a systematic, forensic system revealing "objective" insights into a poem or other works of literature. For the Sputnik-shocked space agers, a methodological approach to criticism had the allure and apparent validity of scientific method, trumping a kind of sloppily subjective reading practice or one derived from the authority of the critic. For an older generation, the study of literature promised a kind of genteel refinement, the acquisition of "taste" as Alexander Pope understood it in his *Essay on Criticism,* the formation of "gentlemen" who could strategically quote Shakespeare and recite chunks of Chaucer and Longfellow. The New Criticism seemed less elitist and more pragmatic: a modern, rationalistic, and democratic approach to literary study.

The children and grandchildren of the boomers find themselves in a different historical moment, when we are overwhelmed by questions about our shared humanity, our efforts to communicate with each other, our mutual survival on the planet. Those questions are made especially urgent by factors such as environmental degradation and the continued oppression and suffering of people throughout the world—particularly those who have been displaced: migrants or refugees. Corresponding with this global crisis has been a transnational wave of extraordinary, visible, and provocative authors in English, addressing these questions poignantly. Collectively, these authors suggest a path forward for traditional programs in literature, many of which are losing students. Postcolonial theory and approaches centering on identity and culture, as well as the interdisciplinary field of ethnic studies, provide a loose intellectual framework from which to organize and promote the study of these authors.

The through line in these origin narratives is a shared conviction that the study of literature will make practitioners better people, but the narratives themselves suggest very different answers about what that would mean. A literary practice that sees the Bible as its originating text and biblical exegesis or hermeneutics—the use of various critical tools to unlock the mysteries and historical truths of foundational literary texts—as its dominant methodology seeks to sort out the "truth" of our canonical texts as reinterpreted in the light of enlightenment rationality. Our interpretive efforts stem from a shared commitment to a set of authoritative texts canonized for their religious value and reinterpreted as a part of the ongoing reexamination of religious faith and meaning. A Classical narrative finds ideal forms in the early literatures of Greece and Rome and defines progress as a kind of spiritual return. There are implicit narratives of greatness and timelessness—the idea that certain authors and texts have transcendent value perceptible by those whose critical skills are sufficiently honed and who are sufficiently dedicated disciples polishing the monuments preserved by their ancestors. This view is romanticized in Ray Bradbury's *Fahrenheit 451:* a cultish set of "handmaids" memorizing and thereby preserving the "mind of the past" (to borrow a phrase from Emerson) for a desolate and apparently doomed generation. It's a powerfully appealing role for the critic: the humble archivist of the past preserving the best of humanity from the destructiveness of the infidels.

Like literary study in general, the profession of ethnic literatures has multiple possible origin stories, some of which I will allude to here. For some, it is a branch of ethnic studies, an interdisciplinary field traceable to the social justice movements of the 1960s and 1970s. One could easily create multiple textual lineages: from Chinua Achebe's *Things Fall Apart* to writers such as Chimamanda Nogozi Adichie and the contemporary explosion in North African fiction, much of it explicitly identifying Achebe's influence; from V. S. Naipaul's *The Mimic Men* to Mohsin Hamid's *The Reluctant Fundamentalist* as examinations of the figure of the migrant confronting colonialist attitudes and Western hegemonic authority; from Jean Rhys's *Wide Sargasso Sea*, widely taught as a companion piece to *Jane Eyre* and emblematic of a shift from a canonical to a postcolonial lens, to Andrea Levy's *Small Island*, which provides its own contrast between one small island (Jamaica) and its colonizing "mother" island; from James Baldwin to Paul Beatty as African American critics of American hypocrisy. This narrative draws on the revolutionary impulse that has always been a part of our writing and reading, an outgrowth, for some, of the Marxist insistence on a literature of social change, of institutional and cultural challenge.

One could similarly create a professional origins narrative from some of the figures who have been monumentalized because of their impact on multiethnic and postcolonial discourse. Gloria Anzaldúa's *Borderlands/La Frontera: The New Mestiza* has retained its interdisciplinary relevance and inspiring power since its publication in 1987 and provides a powerful introduction to the idea of the borderland and liminal identities. Paulo Freire's *Pedagogy of the Oppressed*, with its rejection of the "banking theory" of education, has inspired a critical pedagogy that continues to accompany the professionalization of ethnic literatures. Edward Said's *Orientalism*, another of the most enduring, influential, and controversial works of theory in the field, helped deconstruct and challenge some of the assumptions that had marred critical approaches to the literature and culture of the "other" and reconstruct a burgeoning interest in Middle Eastern literary studies (one of the most fecund and diverse of the emerging international literatures in English).

Another of those foundational influences on the development of ethnic literary study is Gayatri Chakravorty Spivak, whose essay "Can the Subaltern Speak?" helped to frame the development of postcolonial theory. It is yet another mission statement of sorts: we become better people when we listen to the voices of those who had been marginalized. For those of us who profess literature, we have the challenge of helping students internalize the reading experience, to consider their own positions, to kindle curiosity about the places and peoples of the world.

One could create a similar narrative around writers capturing twentieth and early twenty-first century historical moments central to creating a multiethnic history: the literary legacy of the Empire Windrush, the arrival of which in the United Kingdom in 1948 inaugurated—at least symbolically—a slow transformation of British culture and a thousand narratives of migration, adaptation, and survival. Ethnic narratives around 9/11 (and 7/7 in the UK) are as diverse in their points of view and representations of ethnicity as Hamid's aforementioned novel and Jonathan Safran Foer's *Extremely Loud & Incredibly Close*. The Lehman Brothers' collapse and the US economic crisis provide a backdrop for *Behold the Dreamers* by Imbolo Mbue, a powerful story about migration, identity, family, and economics. The novels of Adichie combine historical trauma—the Biafran War, for example, in *Half of a Yellow Sun*—with the personal and collective trauma of migration and the transnational experience. The Obama elections are given an international perspective in NoViolet Bulawayo's *We Need New Names*, as well as in Adichie's *Americanah*. The "Arab Spring" has left a remarkably rich and painful literary record, again with multiple points of view and historical framing.

The risk of citing this handful of writers who I believe constitute an emerging force in literary study is to appear to privilege one author or ethnic literature at the expense of others. The profession of ethnic literatures is a coalition of specialists, each with a discrete focus and theoretical framework, and expertise across the areas of concentration is out of reach for most mere mortals. Specialists in indigenous literatures, South Asian literatures, and the literatures of the Caribbean have commonalities in terms of their professional commitments, ideologies, and (to some extent) training, but the idea of specialist expertise across the different ethnic literatures in English seems as unfeasible as taking on more than one national literature. The central unifying element among these specialists, again, is a sense that all are in the business of making better citizens, of improving human beings and facilitating their communication and shared understanding. The study of literature is a means of working toward social justice and expanding human connection.

The act of selecting those writers who can best foster these goals remains a challenge, and many scholars want to avoid the substitution of one literary canon for another. Writers in English of extraordinary skill are emerging from the Caribbean, from the nations of Africa, from the Middle East, and throughout Asia. The people of the world have found the English language (sometimes in translation) a vehicle for telling stories that might not have been heard or studied when "English" meant British (and sometimes just English) and American literature, the literatures of empire. Some critics of ethnic literature hold on to some formulation of this belief in "greatness" as an inherent and discoverable criterion. Reed Way Dasenbrock writes,

> A work of genuine power will confront us with things we haven't confronted before. That confrontation—no matter what our ethnic identity may be—will cause us to come face-to-face with our own values in a way that will either cause those values to change or cause us to become more aware of them and more reflective about their value. (700)

The critic attempts to define and situate "greatness" in a literary work as a characteristic likely to produce some kind of internal conflict, to require readers to examine the way they engage with other people and cultures. The reading and critical communities we create confront and are confronted by new perspectives and new insights into individual people and their communities. The representative authors I'll feature here have extraordinary strategies for confronting readers who may have little in common with the authors other than a shared language. For example, Hamid, in *The Reluctant Fundamentalist*, holds his reader/auditor captive with his narrative of Princeton education and Wall Street success and summer love, which becomes a narrative of radicalization after 9/11 . . . as the sun sets on an outdoor café in Lahore. The author is able to use his art to force this kind of confrontation, dramatized by the principal characters and enacted with readers themselves.

The idea of ethnic literatures—of literatures concerned with difference, with cultural heritage, with identity, with gender and sexuality, with migration—is an organizing opportunity for a part of English studies in the coming decades. Like the field of ethnic studies, ethnic literary study is interdisciplinary (not always helpful in terms of university funding, but connections among disciplines can be healthy and productive). Students of literature deserve to feel engaged in the world they inhabit, to feel a part of resolving the conflicts that plague us and the mistakes that continue to threaten our existence. They should communicate internationally as readers and scholars. Certainly, I'm making my own value judgment at this point, but I think that creating critical readers and writers who are actively engaged in improving the world is about the best we can hope for as professors of English.

Working in a departmental area and graduate concentration in multicultural and transnational literatures, I have been part of an alliance of specializations that I think characterizes most departments. For my area, it means finding commonality among specialists in African American, Latinx, Indigenous, Caribbean, African, and Asian literatures, among others. Folklore is also one of our components, and film studies as well. Colleagues affiliated with our area offer queer theory, children's literature, and various world literatures. By and large, we are a functional coalition with constantly changing boundaries. In "Frontline Teaching Ruminations, Sober and Hilarious, of an Ethnic Literature Professor," Bonnie TuSmith observes that "anxiety is not only a general feature of our contemporary times but an especially prevalent condition in practitioners of multi-ethnic literary studies" (23). The institutional status of multiethnic literary study has always seemed precarious to me, as it has been for our allies in interdisciplinary studies. And yet we persist.

TuSmith contributes to a special edition of the *MELUS* journal focusing on pedagogy; the organization has been receptive to creative approaches to teaching multiethnic literatures. MELUS is likely the closest our area has to a flagship organization, although its focus is nominally on Multi-Ethnic Literature of the United States. The organization has welcomed research and presentations on a great variety of world authors in English. There was some public debate at the last conference about the usefulness of preserving the "United States" part of the title. For that and other reasons, most of my colleagues go to conferences within their own areas of specialization—as I think literature scholars tend to prefer more specialized conferences to MLA.

In most narratives of origin for the study of ethnic literatures in the United States, the civil rights movement looms large as a moment of creation. The Black Arts Movement—its poetry, drama, fiction, autobiography—inspired a new appreciation of once-ignored works of art. For many in the profession of English living through the revolutionary turbulence, teaching and reading are inevitably bound to the historical present. We had fantasized a space apart, like the Wanamaker Globe, where Wordsworth can always fall madly for Annette Vallon and "a person from Porlock" will always interrupt Coleridge. It's why I wouldn't want to romanticize (pardon the pun) a small set of authors, whose prominence might serve as a barrier to others. Still, Adichie, Bulawayo, Shafak, and Hamid all represent accessible and, for many, appealing ports of entry for the study of transnational literatures in English. They are broadly ambitious in the questions they pose about culture, identity, history, and love. They each have remarkably diversified literary oeuvres. And they have all received enough critical attention that the conversations about them (ongoing in journals, online, and in conference presentations) are a model of active critical engagement with a subject.

## Anxious Times

These are anxious times, indeed. In an earlier reflection on the relationship between literature and literary criticism and their role in the study and profession of English, I returned to Matthew Arnold as one of the progenitors of a century-and-a-half-old tradition of declaiming a crisis in the humanities and warning against a moral crisis in the world at large (Taylor 199–222). I now hearken back to an even earlier voice, that of Alexander Pope, who also tried to reconcile poetry and criticism in a literary culture overrun with pretenders and dunces. It's a return to my earliest professional identity as a specialist in eighteenth-century British literature by way of a poem that may have first turned me in the direction of literary history, Alexander Pope's *Essay on Criticism*.

In the early eighteenth century, the invention of new media such as newspapers and magazines brought new scrutiny to the "world of letters," democratizing writing and authorship to a degree and creating a fraught public relationship between authors and critics. Pope imagines a Classical ideal that had presumably governed that relationship: "Then criticism the Muse's handmaid prov'd, / To dress her charms, and make her more belov'd" (Lines 102–103). To writers such as Pope, the explosion in print that occurred in London, especially during the first decades of the 1700s, must have seemed chaotic and even damaging to those engaged in poetry or to those often self-appointed judges appearing in the growing number of publications dedicated to survey London's new literary "infrastructure," as some have called it.

In this golden age of poetry, at least as Pope and the "neoclassical" imagination appropriated it, the "Muse" offered a unified explanation for the source of writing: a divine inspiration supplied by the nine goddesses of Classical mythology, invoked as a kind of precondition or creative stimulus for the poetic imagination. True poetry must come from a divine source, blessed and spiritualized by this unifying wellspring. True criticism, as Pope defined it, occupied a subservient position: to "improve" the writing as a handmaid attends to a lady preparing herself for public presentation. Naturally, critics then and now have been reluctant to accept this circumscribed role as servant to the muse, and criticism has, at times, been perceived as its own art form, deserving its own centrality rather than a role as a bit player in the creative process.

Pope's prescriptions for poetry and criticism came to represent the so-called Neoclassical period, an aesthetic ideal that provides both a unifying spiritual source for writing and a "correct" critical template for reading and evaluating poetry. It's hardly representative of the world of letters as a whole as it developed in the period, but the impulse was consistent with a larger British fantasy: that Britain would assume the mantle of Roman power and Greek intellectual achievement for the modern era. The model survived, at least theoretically, until Wordsworth and Coleridge created their own unifying fantasy: an aesthetic more "natural" and popular designed to overthrow the supposed artifice of a previous age. Wordsworth and Coleridge's *Lyrical Ballads*, and the work that followed from this new prescription, had a fairly short literary-historical heyday (Victoria's ascension in 1837 usually marks a new era) but a long reach in terms of its influence among readers and writers.

When literature emerged as a subject to be studied in universities and began to assume loose disciplinary configurations, the "profession" of literature and literary criticism again sought meaningful and unifying frameworks, which are part of disciplinary identification. As the titles of some of the remaining literary periodicals from the late nineteenth and early twentieth centuries suggest, scholars tried out the idea of philology as a unifying framework. What united practitioners, presumably, was a shared commitment to understanding language, whether belletristic writing, literary criticism, linguistics, or history and culture. While the term *philology* served for a short time as a convenient umbrella, it was not sufficiently delimiting to help define what later would become English studies, not sufficiently clear in its signification for many in the field. It was hard to say just what a philologist was.

The kinds of narratives suggested by a more purely historical approach proved highly durable and easy to convey or teach. "From Neoclassicism to Romanticism" is the sort of easily trackable shift amenable to graphic lists of characteristics, representative authors, and typical tropes and metaphors. A historical approach to the discipline of English divided its practitioners into Medievalists, Victorianists, Americanists—or perhaps more specifically—American Literary Realists. A fusion of historical periods, aesthetic trends, national boundaries, and genres provided a kind of organizational scheme that was relatively easy to package. Textbooks in literature were designed with these frameworks in mind, as were university curricula and syllabi. Professors and their students were handmaids in the service of one of these periods with the occasional admixture of theory, genre, and varying historical or cultural components.

English studies generally and most university English departments still reflect this disciplinary construction around history and nationality, although for a variety of reasons it's a shadowy reflection of a consensus that has disappeared. One of the engines of change has been an explosion of interest in world literatures in English. The institutional success of cultural studies helped inaugurate a shift away, for many in the discipline, from a principal focus on literary aesthetics to the text as both reflection and instigator of social change. The role of the critic, too, seems to be shifting. Many are no longer content to be handmaids quietly serving a tidily defined discipline, dutiful purveyors of tradition. Increasingly, professors and all of those engaged in literary study have evinced an active engagement with their own cultural present and are not merely standing guard as museum keepers. The social movements that produced civil rights movements and postcolonial theory and exciting literatures in English from all corners of the globe—literatures requiring more than the traditional tools of the aesthetic critic—have led to what might be seen as a new mandate, a new unifying myth: the readers, writers, and critics as advocates and activists for social justice.

The idea of English studies itself is an attempt at unity, as with philology. In spite of our collaborations, conferences, and publications, it remains difficult to conceive of the profession writ-large rather than the structures and debates that have made and remade one's own academic department. If the Modern Language Association once had a tenuous claim to establishing sets of professional standards, there is less of a consensus now on a single flagship organization for English studies; rather, most of us engage professionally at a level of specialization that excludes most other departmental colleagues. We are specialists in eighteenth-century British literature or Latinx literatures, for example—and the conference and publication venues specific to those specializations lay claim to our primary disciplinary attention.

In writing about developments in English studies, Jessica Yood observes, "we are no longer teaching the conflicts, we are experiencing them, as they evolve, in print" (538). Criticism is necessarily an act of social and political engagement, and the authors who comprise this transnational wave are themselves exemplars of movement among cultures, as well as centering their work on the most compelling crises that have informed their own experiences. They invite readers to try to transcend their own national identities, perhaps in the name of creating global citizens. Oliver Goldsmith's "Citizen of the World" was a satirical figure, a naïve engagement through a preposterous "Oriental" persona, making observations about the peculiarities of English culture. The hope for literary transnationalism is to connect readers to the complexity of ethnic identities and cultures and to transcend—to the extent that is possible—the confines of nationalism and the official narratives used to denigrate and control the other. Criticism should be a powerful rhetorical act—potentially a liberatory one: a dialogic participation and engagement with a text and a community of readers.

Because of the uncertainty surrounding our collective sense of our own discipline, the professional narratives designedly support the claims of particular specializations and histories that privilege one area of study over another. A part of any satisfying narrative must be the kinds of negotiations and conflicts that have defined and transformed us. In "Reinventing English Studies," Thomas

Samson describes the uneasy reconciliation among specialists in "language and literature": negativity toward literature was in large part a reaction to the "idealism and elitism in the vociferous demand for a literature-driven language programme" (467–68). While many professionals remain divided, some recognize a necessary link between both areas of expertise and pursue reconciliation or at least a rapprochement.

This kind of divide, of course, not only hints at the relationship between linguistics and literary study but also at the still-uneasy relationship between rhetoric and composition and literature. In practical terms, literature as a field was widely critiqued as elitist and even racist and sexist, while composition is an upstart whose specialists focused on pedagogy, which was not "real" research in the minds of many scholars of literature. Composition specialists shocked their literature colleagues by removing traditional literature from the composition classroom. Literary specialists at many institutions conspired to prevent rhet/comp specialists from gaining tenure. The wounds from those battles have not yet fully healed.

Jeremiads about the imminent death of English as a discipline and particularly the demise of traditional literary study are common and play on our fears about our livelihoods. One of my favorites of these is *Addison and Steele Are Dead* by Brian McCrea (1990), which anticipates complaints about "political correctness" in literary study, the disappearance of "great authors" (however defined), and the distortion of literary history in the service of diversifying the academic curriculum. In spite of the dire predictions, however, English has shown a remarkable durability: In "Who Says English Is a Dying Discipline?," James F. English takes issue with fellow scholars who claim that English studies is declining at a rapid and devastating rate. Instead, English claims that English departments are increasing and holding their own, so to speak, because "English is one of the larger and more durable disciplines in a growing global system." He asserts that we need to "stop writing its obituary and start charting its future," specifically one that will be "increasingly international." So one possible conclusion is that our business in the study of multiethnic literatures is to operate within the traditions of English studies and pull toward the international rather than moving toward a separate disciplinary configuration.

One of the implicit assumptions in Pope's passage cited above is that literature is somehow good for us: "It would communicate to them the moral riches of bourgeois civilization, impress upon them a reverence for middle-class achievements, and, since reading is an essentially solitary, contemplative activity, curb in them any disruptive tendency to collective political action" (Eagleton 22). How many times have I repeated to my Intro to Lit students Horace's "The aim of the poet is to inform or *delight.*" To delight and instruct: I guess part of the "instruct" is this kind of civilizing impulse. Teach students Wordsworth, and they won't participate in food riots. Teach them to respond critically to *Hamlet*, and they'll join the Chamber of Commerce. I do think there is plenty of moral imperative at the root of what we do; how we understand that imperative, though, is the question.

## Reading the Transnational Wave: Four Authors

In a piece for the *Journal of American Studies*, Robert Gross employs the term *transnational turn* in the context of American studies in the aftermath of the *Heath Anthology*, a dramatically more representative or diverse "packaging" of American literature. The appearance of the *Heath Anthology* and its successful replacement of older, whiter, more canonically conservative American literature textbooks seemed to challenge the stability and even the intellectual basis of professing American literature while reflecting a more radical reimagination of America itself. Gross writes, "America is coming to be, not a nationality but a transnationality, a weaving back and forth, with the other lands, of many threads of all sizes and colors" (381). The image of the shuttle here is useful and descriptive of the kinds of strategic interactions this "turn" has effected.

A parallel movement on a broader stage is captured by Paul Jay in *Global Matters: The Transnational Turn in Literary Studies*. Jay sees the confluence of brilliant new narratives from writers throughout the world, some writing in English as their second language and moving between and outside of borders. Maria Koundara helpfully differentiates the terms *transnational* and *multicultural*: the former is distinguished "by its forms, its negotiation of time, and its production of a space that does not nostalgically point either to that of the nation or to a future devoid of nations" (5). It is an extranational arena apart from the concept of national literatures and perhaps distinct from the analysis of postcolonialism, with its concern for the lasting damage done by imperialist nations and the aspirations and challenges of emerging nations.

The emerging body of transnational works reveals some distinctive structural and stylistic features, some of them typical, more generally, of postmodern literature: nonlinear plots, multiple points of view, rejection of a concluding reassertion of providential justice, and an embrace of irresolution and chaos rather than the tidy and presumably reassuring conclusions of previous generations. Beyond these conventions, the works have a number of commonalities in spite of their cultural and geographic diversity. One of these seems to be a preference for the hybrid genre of fictional biography: narratives clearly tied to the author's personal experiences and yet just as clearly fictionalized. Readers worldwide seem now to have relaxed their assumptions about the "truth" of literary memoirs and have generally accepted the poststructural dictum that all narratives are, in one way or another, fundamentally fictive—works of invention that are products of the subjectivity and imagination of their authors.

Another characteristic of this wave of international fiction is self-consciousness about translation and the challenge of moving from one language to another. Authors such as Elif Shafak, who made the shift from writing in Turkish to writing in English, tend to be self-reflexive about the ways language represents culture, and translations tend to be more collaborative than in the past, with translators increasingly assuming the role of literary partners engaging with the essence of the creative process. The success of a transnational work depends on its being amenable to various forms of translation, linguistic and cultural. Often strategic connections to Western readers, with their assumptions and expectations about culture and race, are an essential part of a work's gaining international currency. And so Chimamanda

Ngozi Adichie, in a novel such as *Americanah*, clearly sees her American audience as primary, even though the characters and settings include Nigeria and the United Kingdom; the book directly addresses American prejudices, misunderstandings, and the precise historical moment of the first Obama election.

Another aspect of making these connections across continents and cultures is the prominence of social media, both as narrative motif and, externally, part of the "author myth" and the process of publication and distribution. Through forums like TED Talks, promotional websites, and connections to other prominent figures—Beyonce as a kind of celebrity publicist for Adichie, as an obvious example—authors have greater access to their prospective audience and the possibility of having tighter control over their own critical reception. For most readers, it is rare that the first "meeting" between author and reader occurs in the front matter of a novel. Rather, the ubiquitous presence of social media gathers and illuminates authors and works as it collects other preferences that readers express or reveal, and the related business of awarding literary prizes—perhaps most notably the Man Booker for transnational works—has become integrated with the process of authorial creation and publication. Book reviews are now predominately an online phenomenon, their place in traditional media such as newspapers disappearing rapidly. Obviously, there are a great number of other commonalities in this emerging literature: the nature of migration as a prominent theme, the complexity and intersectionality of identity, the power of home and memory, the experience of "alienation"—all are typically features of the transnational wave. They are often unabashedly political, critiquing globalization and the kind of cruel nationalism that seems to be emerging in the twenty-first century.

As exemplars of the transnational movement, I offer writers such as Shafak, Adichie, Hamid, and NoViolet Bulawayo to represent the phenomenal wave of writers in English whose works and lives transcend national borders. Adichie places herself in an authorial line from Chinua Achebe through Buchi Emecheta, among others. Shafak creates edgy—sometimes deadly—confrontations between past and present, between multiple representations of Turkey and the United Kingdom and even the Southwestern United States. Both Adichie and Shafak have been contributing feminist voices, including strong online presences. Hamid is amazingly inventive, a mesmerizing writer, whose novel *The Reluctant Fundamentalist* has been one of the most enduring of the post-9/11 works of fiction. Bulawayo represents the phenomenal narrative skill possessed by many in the most recent wave of transnational writers and writing. Initially published as a short story, the "Country Games" episode in *We Need New Names* is richly evocative, almost mythic in its invocation of the dreams of suffering children and the devastating poverty in which they grow up.

I don't mean to suggest some sort of canon of mid-career transnational writers. David Palumbo-Liu's collection *The Ethnic Canon* was an extremely helpful framework for faculty members looking to collaborate in teaching and scholarship on ethnic literatures. But the value lies in the idea of framing itself: writers, critics, theorists, and readers discovering and structuring connections among the texts they are studying. Svend Erik Larsen argues that this transnational phenomenon is disrupting conventional practices in literary history that were "embedded in the national paradigm," and he argues that new transnational frameworks are revealing that a "literature does not just *have* a history, but *creates* history" (241). Transnational authors challenge the "official narratives" of history—the Armenian holocaust, 9/11, the consequences of Robert Mugabe's rule in Zimbabwe, the Obama presidency, the crisis in migration that is itself transnational—history reconceived and made fluid through new transtemporal and transnational lenses.

Presumably, authors and critics are creating a new literary history and what Rebecca Walkowitz describes as a new geography of the book. Criticism is not simply about "the places where books are written, but also [about] the places where they are classified and given social purpose" (527). This social purpose is revealed when critics resist the tidy classification of works by a single national history and identity but conceived, rather, as illustrative of our shared humanity and identities that are mutable and infinitely complex.

Rodica Mihaila cites a number of global factors that have been responsible for this shift toward new paradigms of literary study: the acceleration of globalization in recent decades; the emergence of cultural studies; the rise of identity politics and border studies; and the pace of disciplinary change and instability in the fields of American literature, comparative literature, and world literature as traditionally configured. Mihaila writes,

> The dynamics of canon formation shows that American literature changes spectacularly when read in a transnational perspective, across the borders of the nation and beyond the tropes of exceptionalism, that is, when read as hemispheric, multilingual, planetary or world literature and it also highlights the dramatic change in post–Cold War American literature produced by the massive infusion of new writers who are migrants or belong to the first generation of migrants' children born in the US. (42)

Peter Morgan defines multiculturalism in literature as referring

> to the works written within a country by writers from different ethno-cultural backgrounds and/or immigrant origins, but within the framework of the national paradigm of literature. This was the 'national' literature of those who had adopted the country as immigrants, primarily, or their immediate offspring who shared a sense of origins in another ethno-national environment. (5)

The transnational wave represents an "emergence of new ways of understanding the parameters of nation and identity in literature" (6). Literary transnationalism, then, is an opportunity for critically mediating national literatures and critically examining the effects of globalization. It is an answer, in part, to the fetishizing tendencies of "Orientalism," the appropriation of "exotic" cultural practices—from the standpoint of the Western imagination—the erasure of the people and their "Eastern" worlds subsumed in the myth of Western rationality and superiority.

## The Bastard of Istanbul

Shafak's *The Bastard of Istanbul* was, for me, a gift from a Turkish exchange student studying in the multicultural and transnational literatures concentration in the English department in which I work. It became one of my favorites to teach because of its sense of history and culture and their intersections. The novel is likely Shafak's best known, associated with her running afoul of the Turkish government in her approach to the Armenian holocaust, and with a matriarchal family playing parts in a tragicomedy.

As a representative transnational novel, *The Bastard of Istanbul* acts as an antidote to complaints about stereotypical characters in fiction, as a further illustration of the worldwide impact of social media—and foremost as a slightly bent take on postmodern existence in relation to history and cultural expectation. Turkey is a bit of an outlier in terms of Middle Eastern studies, although it has been part of the purview of traditional "Orientalism." It has a fraught relationship with Europe and also political and religious connections to various Middle Eastern cultures. Its history with the Armenian genocide (which began in 1915) and its stubborn—almost pathological—denial (a kind of Holocaust denial) is taken up by contemporary writers at their peril.

*The Bastard of Istanbul* is a novel about blame, blame in a historical context, as it's bandied about in the twin cafes in the novel, the Café Constantinopolis and the Café Kundera. Historical trauma, whether of seventy years ago or a hundred or three hundred or even two thousand, defines much of human history and much of modern life. It is part of identity, culture, and the stories that define us. Here, of course, it has parallels in the individual lives of the characters, and it is enmeshed in secret family histories. This is a book about secrets as well as trauma.

There is a tremendous irony in the book—which is, indeed, one layer of coincidence upon another: the Turkish family, the Kazancıs, is connected to the Armenian family, the Tchakmakhchians, in ways that neither group anticipated. To me, this represents another powerful historical phenomenon that I think we're only beginning to come to grips with: we are all connected; all of our stories and family histories interlock in stunning ways. "Life is coincidence, though sometimes it takes a djinni to fathom that" (Shafak, *Bastard* 356).

One of the features this novel shares with many others coming from younger transnational authors, as I've suggested, is the centrality of social media and the subversive possibilities inherent in worldwide communication. Because of the Internet and in this case because of social networking groups established online, the descendants—both Turkish and Aremenian—of this ethnic cleansing can communicate with each other and discover such dangerous national and international secrets.

Novels such as *Bastard* and some of Shafak's others, such as *The Forty Rules of Love* (with Rumi as a historical character) and *The Architect's Apprentice*, interweave past and present, with resultant collisions that are revelatory and disruptive. *Honour* is among her grimmest works: a painful novel about honor killing in London. It is one of the few novels in which the city of Istanbul is not essentially a main character. Here, the practice of honor killing is shown as a transnational phenomenon, an implicit argument for an international feminism that asserts the fundamental rights of women across cultural boundaries. In her prose work, Shafak has become an increasingly visible spokesperson for what she frequently calls a global sisterhood and a movement advocating for women's rights that transcends Western ideologies and national borders. In her recent TED Talk, she advocates for "the revolutionary power of diverse thought." Perhaps this claim, as applied to the study of multiethnic literatures, suggests a kind of revolutionary spirit directed toward social justice throughout the world that might underlie our professional engagements as scholars, instructors, and readers. Shafak's readers become apostles for the transforming and subversive power of diversity.

## *Mohsin Hamid and His Magic Doors*

Mohsin Hamid is another prominent member of the transnational wave. With writers such as Shafak, Adichie, Bulawayo, Khaled Hosseini, Junot Díaz, and Imbolo Mbue, he is finding crossover audiences for his work dramatizing human migration and its effect on human experience and its broader cultural implications. These authors are making their presence felt at a time of political peril and extraordinary xenophobia; they are writing into a headwind of political opportunism and ethnic violence. Their voices are well represented online—for example, in debates about world feminism—and for both academic and nonacademic readers, they present a perspective on the human cost of racism and violence otherwise inaccessible or unrepresented. The remarkable literary talent emerging in places such as Pakistan, for example, provides a counternarrative to the images that construct these places in the popular Western imagination.

The transnational movement in fiction has complicated our sense of place. In this respect, Hamid's latest novel *Exit West* is a fulfillment of a larger pattern in his use of setting and an increasing ambiguity concerning location and even ethnic identity. His first novel, *Moth Smoke*, is set in Lahore; it's a satire that is specifically Pakistani. *The Reluctant Fundamentalist* is set partly in Lahore with an unidentified American and a mysterious narrator who tells a largely American tale, echoing the likes of F. Scott Fitzgerald, but with international movement and implication. The setting for *How to Get Filthy Rich in Rising Asia* remains obscure except as a place conforming to this notion of "rising Asia"—at the level of allegory but identifying markers of place have been erased in the narrative. It's a satire, again, self-consciously transnational or perhaps extranational. *Exit West* also employs an unspecific setting for the narrative framework, although the protagonists are clearly living in a period of devastating insecurity in a war-torn, ethnically divided city. But about one-third of the way through the book, Hamid disrupts geography more fundamentally than he has in the past: by magically bypassing it.

On one level, Hamid's novels are love stories—the lovers beset by some sort of dysfunction either personal or social—so "the course of true love never did run smooth" and in fact usually fizzles or dissipates in time. And so in *Exit West*, Nadia and Saeed are the sweethearts, both of them informed by their conservative religious heritage, although both of them rebellious, too, in different ways. They are themselves transitional figures, letting go of a past represented by dying parents and a disintegrating political environment. Aside from its geographic non-specificity, it's a mostly realistic novel for the first one-third of its pages.

The door as magical device is first presented as a product of war and the desperation of refugees and those trapped in the violence. Actually, before he introduces the device, the author foreshadows this magical transformation with his comment about the meaning of windows in wartime: "One's relationship to windows now changed in the city. A window was the border through which death was possibly most likely to come" (49). The window is, of course, a means of ingress and egress, as well as a visual connection to the outside, a means of letting in light. Windows represent vulnerability, and broken windows mean chaos and the threat of death.

As the war intensifies, the author turns to the matter of doors:

> The effect doors had on people altered as well. Rumors had begun to circulate of doors that could take you elsewhere, often to places far away, well removed from this death trap of a country. Some people claimed to know people who knew people who had been through such doors. A normal door, they said, could become a special door, and it could happen without warning, to any door at all. Most people thought these rumors to be nonsense, the superstitions of the feeble-minded. But most people began to gaze at their own doors a little differently nonetheless. (72)

This transformation of door to magic portal begins in rumor and superstition, a product of fear and desperation. But as with the windows, the effects of war begin to alter people's relationship with these exits that are simultaneously entrances. Somehow, in this dystopian vision, fantasy is made real.

Hamid has taken readers to the realm of science fiction, of supernatural dystopia. It's a shocking turn initiated by the "twinge of irrational possibility" (Hamid 73), an apparently convenient and easy *deus ex machina* that will rescue the lovers and all those suffering around them and deliver them into what might seem like a borderless world out of John Lennon's "Imagine."

There have been no happily-ever-afters in the Hamid canon so far. The protagonists Nadia and Saeed maintain a tangential connection to each other. They even hold a late-in-life reunion of sorts. But they don't find true love, nor do they find a new home. Their lives, the reader is led to believe, will remain transient, disconnected, in a kind of permanent liminality.

The author makes a claim for the universality of the migrant experience: "Everyone migrates, even if we stay in the same houses our whole lives, because we can't help it. We are all migrants through time" (131). The passage of time renders all of us culturally adrift, homeless. Aging entails an inevitable alienation. In one fashion or another, to be human is to be a migrant.

None of Hamid's novels can be reduced to a simple moral imperative or political message. His work is, by turns, environmental literature, science fiction, romance, bildungsroman, anti-war, anti-colonialist—all of it fashioned into a brilliant and visceral economy of language and metaphor. Because he is such a careful stylist and is increasingly conscious of his place in the world of letters, the risk of creating a magical device at the core of his work of fiction becomes apparent. Some have already slapped on the obvious label so often applied to postcolonial and transnational fiction: magical realism.

In some respects, the term could apply to this novel: it represents global economic forces perpetuating colonization and contrasts the magical (commonly understood to represent colonized people) and the real (the colonizers). The novel almost casually juxtaposes a realistic narrative and a supernatural device with the expectation that the reader will easily suspend disbelief. And yet the term is reductive and so is usually rejected by authors and critics not wanting to comply with whatever expectations are attached to being a "postcolonial" writer. Anyway, Hamid has already established a history of subverting and even mocking literary genres in his novels, and I believe that may be part of his decision to introduce a magical element in this novel. It is a deliberate deception, as *Rising Asia* is at least in appearance a self-help book and rags-to-riches story. It is neither, although it satirizes both bits of popular Western cultural history.

In his movement towards allegory and a tendency toward universalizing, Hamid is fashioning an everyman, an everywoman, and an everyplace—a chaos of ethnic anxiety and violence. It is a bleak vision, and yet the author's faith in shared human experience and our ability to communicate at least something about that experience remains powerful. At a time when powerful people are demonizing and dehumanizing migrants, Hamid allows the reader to inhabit characters who are both representative and strikingly individualized in a crisis dramatized in frighteningly realistic detail and a magical device that offers only an illusory escape. The book asks its readers to do more than suspend disbelief but also to see in the suffering humanity of its migrant characters a reflection of the broader human condition. More than the sort of empathy that comes easily to readers safely removed from the wartime inferno many in the world experience, the novel prompts us to remember that we are all migrants and will share a common fate.

## *Obama-Era America in Adichie's* Americanah *and Bulawayo's* We Need New Names

I pair two novels, one by Adichie and one by Bulawayo, in part because they both capture an overlapping historical moment, the United States of the Obama-era America and the jubilant response throughout the world (including hyberbolic declarations of a "postracial" America and compelling and difficult national conversations about race). These two writers also provide a sharp contrast. Adichie is an established and highly successful novelist with popular culture recognition via Beyoncé's video that quotes her, her oft-cited TED Talks, and an online discourse about women's rights and feminism. Bulawayo, by contrast, has had one major success as a novelist, but one that indicates she is an ingenious craftsperson with a unique perspective. Her Zimbabwe is incomparably distinct from Adichie's Nigeria, and the hardships and humiliations Adichie's Ifemelu must endure are utterly different from the American migrant experience of Darling, Bulawayo's protagonist, who is shocked by what she experiences as a newcomer living in "Destroyed, Michigan."

Both of these writers provide stunning insights into race, class, gender, and geography in a remythologized contemporary America. As new inhabitants in places as disparate as New Haven and Detroit, their protagonists are transformed as they try to survive in a landscape that threatens to consume them and obliterate their fading sense of "home." Both writers interrogate this storied landscape now governed by a president of African heritage, and both struggle desperately to navigate and simultaneously critique its peculiar constructions of identity.

Both works are clearly written for Western and African audiences, and that sense of a double-readership poses narrative problems for authors trying to speak truthfully about this land of dreams to which their protagonists have come and in which they have suffered. As much as these novels have in common, differences in their portrayal of transnational experiences shed light on representations of poverty, sexuality, and memory that inform our sense of the contemporary "transnational turn" and new and unsettling portraits of an America seen through the ideas of some of its newest immigrants.

One striking commonality in these novels, both of which are based loosely on the authors' own experiences as travelers and immigrants, is that they incorporate the election of President Barack Obama as an important plot element. Both authors, through their protagonists, provide insight into what the election of an African American president might mean. Bulawayo explains what this election means to a teenager who'd left the poverty of Robert Mugabe's Zimbabwe and the violence surrounding the contested election of 2008, which serves as a counterpoint to Obama's first presidential election. And in Adichie's novel, the protagonist's blog posts, interwoven with the narrative of her protagonist's experiences, use the election as one of the centerpieces for her exploration of the meaning of race in America or, as she puts it, "learning to be black."

In *We Need New Names*, the reader meets Bulawayo's protagonist Darling as a ten-year-old who distinguishes herself from her fellow marauders—all displaced from school and more or less fending for themselves—as the one with great prospects: "I'll be living in America with Aunt Fostalina, eating real food and doing better things than stealing [guavas]" (12). Her partner-in-crime, named Bastard, is wearing a Cornell t-shirt (14), a sly allusion to the misguided American benevolence that has damaged the local clothing industry. He warns her presciently, "What if you get there, and find it's a kaka place and get stuck and can't come back?" (16). Darling's Aunt Fostalina is already in America working in a nursing home; or, as Bastard puts it, she is "busy cleaning kaka off some wrinkled old man who can't do anything for himself" (17).

Fostalina lives in some mysterious place they call "Destroyedmichygen." The misheard city name may be the first indication that all will not be dreamy in this dream land. The children play "country-game," a kind of geopolitical hopscotch. "Everybody wants to be the U.S.A." (61) in this game, and the children's own country is one of the least desirable choices. When the NGO lorry comes with its resupply of Western t-shirts, the children instruct the workers: "Next time: shoes, All Stars, balls, cell phones, cake, underwear, drinks, biscuits, U.S. dollars" (58). Instead, they get Google t-shirts and toy guns. "We take off and run to kill each other with our brand-new guns from America" (59). So America is a place of real food, and all stars, and cell phones, and dollars, and guns. The reader also learns about the requirements of political leadership: "You know one day I'll become president, Bastard says"; "You have to be an old, old man" (62); and "Presidents are very rich" (63).

When Darling has moved to "Destroyedmichygen," almost everything defies her expectations, including Bastard's lessons in political science:

> On TV that pretty man Obama who has been saying, Yes We Can, America, Yes We Can, is becoming president. He does not look old like our own president; he looks maybe like our president's child. There are crowds and crowds of white people and black people and brown people, just people, and they are happy and cheering and clapping. (158)

The election of Obama is a powerful counterlesson to the other lessons she's learning about being dark-skinned in America, the ludicrous stereotypes surrounding the American conception of being African: "You are in America now and you can actually be anything you want to be, look at Obama" (160).

Here the Obama election seems to suggest that America might be, after all, a place of opportunity, of infinite promise. And yet the rest of her narrative does not bear out the optimism surrounding the 2008 US election. One of her mates, Stina—like Bastard—had warned Darling that "a country is a Coca-Cola bottle that can smash on the floor and disappoint you. When a bottle smashes, you cannot put it back together" (162). Her America, the one she experiences in Destroyedmichygen and its environs, is a land of Coke bottle shards. She writes, "In America we saw more food than we had seen in all our lives and we were so happy we rummaged through the dustbins of our souls to retrieve the stained, broken pieces of God" (240). And yet after eating all the Big Macs and Chinese buffets, they find themselves classified as "illegals," despised, brutally marginalized, hated—and perhaps worst of all for Darling, stuck in America, as her memories of Zimbabwe and her old sense of self recede from her grasp.

It is a primal and deeply wounding picture of disillusionment. And painfully, President Obama is a figure of disillusionment for Darling: the youthful, optimistic, dark-skinned hero who will transform this soulless landscape. But the broken pieces of God are not to be found here, and Darling will apparently remain in a kind of spiritual limbo between her birthplace and this new brand of spiritual poverty.

Adichie's narrative is strikingly different, mostly a function of the economic and social background of her protagonist, Ifemelu, who leaves Nigeria for the privileged environment of the American Ivy Leagues. The reader first learns the term *Americanah* in the context of the political oppression academics face in Nigeria, a theme prevalent in Adichie's earlier novels as well. An Americanah is one who returns from a trip to the United States with snobbery and affected speech, rather like British complaints in the eighteenth century about young people returning from their grand tours of Europe. In this derogatory term is embedded the notion that travel to America changes people and not for the better—it makes them ill-fitted to return to their old lives as Nigerians. Adichie alludes to President Obama throughout the novel. The first mention of the 2008 election occurs when Ifemelu is living in New Haven with her boyfriend of three years, Blaine. The two had quarreled, but "They survived that fight, mostly because of Barack Obama, bonding anew over their shared passion. On election night, before Blaine kissed her, his face wet with tears, he held her tightly as though Obama's victory was also their personal victory" (3). The stunning electoral victory and its aftermath serve as a centerpiece in the author's ongoing exploration of race in America, especially in the context of the naïve proclamations of a "postracial" society that would somehow follow in the wake of Obama's victory.

Ifemelu's experiences in America mirror those of Darling in terms of the starkness of the "education in race" she receives, the stereotyped "Africanness" she observes, and the disillusionment she feels, although her education and class, at least to a certain extent, seem to shield her from the cruelest sorts of oppression that some immigrants to America experience. Through the mechanism of the blog, she finds both an outlet for her intellectual exploration and also a personal voice. She writes, "Dear Non-American

Black, when you make the choice to come to America, you become black. Stop arguing. Stop saying I'm Jamaican or I'm Ghanaian. America doesn't care. So what if you weren't 'black' in your country? You're in America now" (222). And then, when she returns to Nigeria, she reports back to Blaine, "Race doesn't really work here. I feel like I got off the plane in Lagos and stopped being black" (475). In Adichie's novel, as in Bulawayo's, race is entirely contingent: a geopolitical fiction that one must necessarily accept and adapt to. Adichie's protagonist, though, can go home, and she can even—in an uncharacteristically romantic ending—reunite with the man who got away. For Darling, though, there is no more home, no possibility of a return.

Adichie's protagonist becomes a well-known blogger as she tries to interpret the meaning of race in America. Her posts show an increasingly nuanced and daring insight, as when she queries her readers: "Why Dark-Skinned Black Women—Both American and Non-American—Love Barack Obama"; "when white people say dark they mean Greek or Italian but when black people say dark they mean Grace Jones" (216);

> Many successful American black men have white wives. Those who deign to have black wives have light (otherwise known as high yellow) wives. And this is the reason dark women love Barack Obama. He broke the mold! He married one of their own. He knows what the world doesn't seem to know: that dark black women totally rock. They want Obama to win because maybe finally somebody will cast a beautiful chocolate babe in a big-budget rom-com that opens in theatres all over the country, not just three artsy theatres in New York City. (217)

And she taps into persistent stereotypes and, in a sense, identifies what the author might perceive as a problem the president has faced throughout his presidency: "Obama Can Win Only If He Remains the Magic Negro" . . . "the black man who is eternally wise and kind. He never reacts under great suffering, never gets angry, is never threatening. He always forgives all kinds of racist shit. He teaches the white person how to break down the sad but understandable prejudice in his heart. You see this man in many films. And Obama is straight from central casting" (322).

This fantasy was, in a sense, enacted in the White House "have a beer together" meeting between Professor Henry Louis Gates and the cop who arrested him for breaking into his own house. The president was a figure of forgiveness, of a desire for unity. The (for many) painfully wrenching end of that era and the chaotic and menacing era in which we seem enmeshed are almost too difficult to acknowledge. But both of these authors remain as constrasting but prescient voices such as are desperately needed.

## A Literature of Engagement

As I write this, the Carolinas have experienced a devastating storm, Hurricane Florence, which brought the region to a frightened halt. It's a ritual humbling those of us in the area endure too frequently and sometimes results in suffering and loss. As the flood waters recede, we reach out to reconnect and reschedule. The storms weigh disproportionately on those who are most vulnerable, but we are all implicated, all enshrouded by the same storm clouds. There will be stories told, poems published, photographs gathered that record stories about this hurricane as there were for Hurricane Floyd, the area's last great tap on the shoulder. It strikes me that this is one kind of literary engagement.

The flourishing of transnational authorship in English represents another kind of opportunity for critical engagement; stories about the movement of people across cultures and across borders offer a complex exchange for narrator and reader. On a scale so large as to be nearly invisible, they communicate in ways that circumvent the official narratives and stereotypes. Imaginative readers, writers, and critics ought to be involved in saving the world. Even if we're not "unacknowledged legislators," readers, writers, and the communities they forge have a role to play in framing all kinds of public debates, often embedded thematically in works of art. To be an advocate for the story as an essential ingredient in our humanity strikes me as a worthy aim. Because so many of the issues confronting humanity are now universal or nearly so, a global approach to literary study dramatizes the process of forging connections.

One of the pleasures of traditional literary history is the experience of temporal reach, of a kind of time travel in which, bit by bit, the explorer gains a bit more of a foothold in a literary past. I wouldn't deny anyone that experience, and I wouldn't suggest that Chaucer or Joyce or Oliver Goldsmith be rendered invisible as museum pieces. But a similar pleasure and one required by the anxious world in which we study and profess is the geographical and cultural reach offered by world literatures. I'm tempted to add "especially those literatures from historically oppressed or marginalized peoples." World literature, as long construed, created a Classical narrative that supports the subsequent literatures of empire while ignoring the voices of colonized, exploited, and unrepresented people.

Literary study and criticism can function as a vibrant agent of outreach and contemporary relevance, asking difficult questions about justice and identity and all of the urgent life concerns dominating our own and our students' lives. There is something comforting about the idea of literary study as a kind of refuge, a place of permanence and appreciation, and the delights that can accompany obscure knowledge. But for many, literature can represent an engagement with the present, with the Other, with the dislocations of cultural difference. These elements should be an integral part of English studies.

Let me conclude by heartily endorsing the seven principles enumerated in the introduction to this study. Disciplinary change is an inevitability that ought to be embraced as evidence of the vitality of our work and our collaborations. Our expanding sense of what constitutes literature, as well, gives students a chance to develop their own judgments about the texts that are most relevant to their own lives and times rather than a devotion to the choices and boundaries established by our distant forebears. Literary study has suffered, I believe, from its own insularity, its arrogant separation from the larger world around it. And we have had the amazing fortune to be joined institutionally with others who share our love of language; our diverse approaches and toolsets should represent creative opportunities for renewed collaboration rather than segregation as rivals for resources and reward.

## Works Cited

Adichie, Chimamanda Ngozi. *Americanah*. Knopf, 2013.

Anzaldúa, Gloria. *Borderlands/La Frontera: The New Mestiza*. Aunt Lute Books, 1987.

Bérubé, Michael. *The Employment of English: Theory, Jobs, and the Future of Literary Studies*. New York UP, 1997.

Bulawayo, NoViolet. *We Need New Names*. Little, Brown, 2013.

Dasenbrock, Reed Way. "Why Read Multicultural Literature? An Arnoldian Perspective." *College English*, vol. 61, no. 6, July 1999, pp. 691–701.

Eagleton, Terry. *Literary Theory: An Introduction*, 3rd ed., U of Minnesota P, 1996.

English, James F. "Who Says English Is a Dying Discipline?" *The Chronicle of Higher Education*, Sept. 2012, https://chronicle.com/article/Who-Says-English-Is-a-Dying/134410/.

Gross, Robert. "The Transnational Turn: Rediscovering American Studies in a Wider World." *Journal of American Studies*, vol. 34, no. 3, Dec. 2000, pp. 373–93.

Hamid, Mohsin. *Exit West*. Penguin, 2017.

———. *The Reluctant Fundamentalist*. Harcourt, 2007.

Jay, Paul. *Global Matters: The Transnational Turn in Literary Studies*. Cornell UP, 2010.

Koundoura, Maria. *Transnational Culture, Transnational Identity: The Politics and Ethics of Culture Exchange*. I. B. Tauris, 2012.

Larsen, Svend Erik. "From the National to a Transnational Paradigm: Writing Literary Histories Today." *European Review*, vol. 21, no. 2, 2013, pp. 241–51.

McComiskey, Bruce, editor. *English Studies: An Introduction to the Discipline(s)*. NCTE, 2006.

McCrea, Brian. *Addison and Steele Are Dead: The English Department, Its Canon, and the Professionalization of Literary Criticism*. U Delaware P, 1990.

Mihaili, Rodica. "Opening the Boundaries of National Literatures: From a Multicultural to a Transnational Literary Canon. The American Challenge." *The Canonical Debate Today: Crossing Disciplinary and Cultural Boundaries*, edited by Liviu Papadima, David Damrosch, and Theo D'haen, Brill, 2011, pp. 39–53.

Morgan, Peter. "Literary Transnationalism: A Europeanist Perspective." *Journal of European Studies*, vol. 47, no. 1, 2017, pp. 3–20.

Palumbo-Liu, David, editor. *The Ethnic Canon: Histories, Institutions, and Interventions*. U of Minnesota P, 1995.

Papadima, Liviu, David Damrosch, and Theo D'haen, editors. *The Canonical Debate Today: Crossing Disciplinary and Cultural Boundaries*. Brill, 2011.

Pope, Alexander. "An Essay on Criticism." *Poetry and Prose of Alexander Pope*, edited by Aubrey Williams, Houghton Mifflin, 1969, pp. 37–57.

Samson, Thomas. "Reinventing English Studies." *English Studies*, vol. 91, no. 4, June 2010, pp. 467–73.

Shafak, Elif. *The Bastard of Istanbul*. Viking Adult, 2006.

———. "The Revolutionary Power of Diverse Thought," TED Talk, 2017, https://www.ted.com/talks/elif_shafak_the_revolutionary_power_of_diverse_thought

Spivak, Gayatri Chakravorty. *The Death of a Discipline*. Columbia UP, 2005.

———. "Can the Subaltern Speak?" *Colonial Discourse and Postcolonial Theory: A Reader*, edited by Patrick Williams and Laura Chrisman, Columbia UP, 1994, pp. 66–111.

Taylor, Richard C. "Literature and Literary Criticism" *English Studies: An Introduction to the Discipline(s)*, edited by Bruce McComiskey, NCTE, 2006, pp. 199–222.

TuSmith, Bonnie. "Frontline Teaching: Ruminations, Sober and Hilarious, of an Ethnic Literature Professor." *MELUS: Multi-Ethnic Literature of the United States*, vol. 42, no. 4, 2017, pp. 20–36.

Walkowitz, Rebecca. L. "The Location of Literature: The Transnational Book and the Migrant Writer." *Contemporary Literature*, vol. 47, no. 4, winter 2006, pp. 527–45.

Yood, Jessica. "Writing the Discipline: A Generic History of English Studies." *College English*, vol. 65, no. 5, 2003, pp. 526–40.

CHAPTER FIVE

# *Critical Theory and Cultural Studies*

JEFFREY J. WILLIAMS
*Carnegie Mellon University*

## I. From Scholarship to Criticism to Theory

By the 1980s, "theory" became the primary practice in literary studies. Before that, literary scholars claimed scholarship or criticism as their main practice, but by the mid-1980s, J. Hillis Miller could declare, in his 1986 presidential address to the central professional organization of literary scholars, the Modern Language Association (MLA), "The Triumph of Theory." Criticism and scholarship did not disappear, but theory designated the various conceptual approaches, schools, or frameworks that scholars espoused, such as structuralism, deconstruction, feminism, psychoanalysis, Marxism, or reader response. The rise of theory enjoined a great deal of controversy, with eminent figures such as Yale's René Wellek proclaiming it was "destroying literary studies" and Harvard's Walter Jackson Bate bemoaning that it caused a crisis in English studies because it seemed to usurp the role of literature, forging a speculative pursuit in its own right and introducing obscure terms and concepts. Most scholarship and criticism took a service position in relation to literature—a historical scholar, for example, might track down the root of a word or the historical source of a detail in one of Shakespeare's plays, providing a footnote to the play, or a literary critic might present a reading of clothing imagery in that play, elaborating a motif of the play. But a theorist might speculate on language, culture, or society in general, as well as comment on literary works.

By 1990, theory was something that those in English studies were expected to know to participate in the discipline, even if to disagree with it, and it took a central position especially in graduate education, the subject of required courses such as Critical Methods, Twentieth-Century Criticism and Theory, or Introduction to the Profession, as well as in individual seminars.[1] The rule of thumb is that as an undergraduate, you are expected to learn about different literary periods, fields, and genres, whereas in graduate school you are expected to learn the discourse and frameworks by which professional scholars address literature. A wave of new textbooks—such as Hazard Adams and Leroy Searle's influential anthology *Critical Theory since 1965*—introductions, and guides published from the 1980s onward presented that discourse, surveying the positions, schools, and main players of theory. Alongside them, a fleet of new journals explicitly devoted to theory emerged through the 1970s and 1980s, transposing the central forums of the field from scholarly or critical matters to theoretical ones.[2]

"Theory" covers an umbrella of activities, but during the 1970s and 1980s, it was often called "literary theory" to distinguish it as something literary critics did, in contrast to what sociologists or economists or psychologists did, who promulgated theories often quite different from what those in literature employed. Some literary theorists looked to psychoanalysis, for example, as a model for uncovering hidden meaning, whereas those in psychology were developing cognitive theory and neurobiology. Theory was also sometimes called "critical theory" to designate that it reflected on the methods that critics use. In a common metaphor, theory comprised a toolbox for doing critical work. A critic, for instance, might take a Marxist frame to focus on class, labor, and economic systems represented in literature, whereas a formalist might be more concerned about the patterns of plot, and a feminist critic might underscore the representation of gender, particularly tacit biases against women. In general, the appellation of "critical theory" suggested a critique of previous ways of thinking, and theory was sometimes announced as a revolution in thought, although its politics varied—some schools, like feminism and Marxism, were explicitly critical of contemporary society, while others, like structuralism, deconstruction, and reader response, largely commented on literary, linguistic, or interpretive matters.[3]

Although theory became the primary shorthand for the work that literary scholars do, it is important to recognize that other kinds of work continued apace. Indeed, since its formation as a discipline in the late 1800s, English has been a capacious field encompassing different tasks, sometimes competing but more often coexisting with some doing historical scholarship, others linguistics, some doing critical interpretations of works, others writing pedagogy, a fair number doing appreciations or creative writing, and some aesthetics or philosophy. The most prominent task of the field from its beginnings through the first half of the twentieth century was "scholarship"—meaning literary history, source studies, or philological scholarship. A literary scholar might study, say, the Latin sources of English Renaissance poetry. Or theater production, laws, and circumstances in Shakespeare's time. Or etymologies of words, in a discipline that is still called philology. To be sure, not everyone did historical scholarship. Some professors argued for the appreciation of literature with florid descriptions of its pleasures rather than the intricate if sometimes pedantic unfolding of a word root. Some professors advocated simply reading literature aloud, believing that scholarship or criticism ruined it, and they held that the best approach was only to experience it, like a splendid sunset.

One can find a snapshot of the era in the American novelist Frank Norris's 1896 essay, "The 'English Courses' of the University of California," about his time at Berkeley (which was the only campus in the system at the time). He complained that English professors only taught students to compile classifications of literary works rather than paying attention to the pleasure or power of the literature itself. While Norris's description of academic scholarship does make it sound tedious—if you major in English, you usually do so because you love poems or particular authors, not because you want to count verb forms or classify types—such a method was a way to establish literary study as a science, like biology, suitable for an academic discipline rather than merely a casual activity, like a conversation one might have with friends after seeing a movie.

English and other language studies were new disciplines—the MLA was founded in 1883 and was very small—so literary scholars aimed to establish their credibility by modeling their pursuit on the classics, the study of ancient Greek and Latin, which had scholarly traditions going back to the Middle Ages. Indeed, a number of early scholars in English argued for the adoption of standards of the study of ancient Greek to English literature, drawing on the principles of philology with scientific protocols of evidence and proof (see Brandt, for instance). While this legitimated the professional study of English, it also made literary scholars look at British, American, and other literatures as distant historical traditions, like ancient Greek, rather than as modern ones, and English studies at the time centered on texts largely from Old and Middle English and the Renaissance. Those constituted the dominant fields in English studies at the time, perhaps extending to eighteenth-century literature. You needed the work of scholars to understand Old English, which is essentially a foreign language and represents an ancient world, or Renaissance literature, which often uses archaic forms and language and represents a historically distant sensibility. According to the literary scholar and critic M. H. Abrams, it was not until the 1950s that literary scholars started looking at Romanticism as a viable field to study. Before that, it was considered to be too modern, literature that undergraduates might be enthused about (and many students memorized poems like Keats's "Ode on a Grecian Urn" at the time) but that did not require scholarly aid to understand.

That started changing during the 1930s and 1940s, as some argued for a more significant place for criticism. One can see the shift in two essays by R. S. Crane, a leading scholar of eighteenth-century British literature at midcentury and a central figure in a group of critics at the University of Chicago, sometimes called the Chicago School or the neo-Aristotelian critics because they took the model of Aristotle's *Poetics* to comment on the forms of literature. In his 1935 essay, "History versus Criticism in the Study of Literature," Crane petitioned for a place at the academic table for criticism—the explication and interpretation of individual works, which had otherwise been relegated to teaching or left to reviews in magazines and newspapers. Within two decades, that turned around, as Crane recounts in his 1957 essay, "Criticism as Inquiry; or, The Perils of the 'High Priori Road," in which he remarks that perhaps the petition succeeded too well, as criticism had become the dominant pursuit at the expense of historical scholarship.

Around the same time, the poet and critic John Crowe Ransom issued a manifesto for "Criticism, Inc." He argued that criticism generated a unique knowledge other disciplines did not. In the context of the expanding university and its competing departments of knowledge—alongside English's emergence as an academic field, most other current disciplines, such as sociology, economics, or psychology, also arose around 1900—literary studies offered knowledge of specifically literary attributes. Ransom did not rule out other pursuits, like history, but ceded it to that department. If you wanted to find out about it, you would look to a professional historian; or if you were concerned about the creative process of an author, you might look to psychology. But the study of literary attributes was something those from other disciplines did not do. To assure criticism's professional legitimacy, he also emphasized an "objective" stance toward literary works, as one might take in a science, ruling out softer procedures such as appreciation or biography. A biologist presumably gives his or her objective understanding of trees rather than describing the pleasure of their shade.

In a 1941 book, Ransom named what became a leading branch of criticism "the New Criticism," which typically focused on metaphors, imagery, or other formal features in particular literary works, and he also founded and edited the leading journal of criticism of the era, *Kenyon Review*. However, it is important to recognize that there were a number of different veins of criticism at the time. For instance, the Chicago School also advocated a kind of formalism but looked more to general types and opposed the New Critics' narrow focus, and the New York Intellectuals were more interested in the social and moral significance of literature. Giving a sense of its range, a leading midcentury survey of criticism, Stanley Edgar Hyman's *The Armed Vision*, inventories at least ten types, including Marxist, archetypal, folk, and biographical approaches, as well as the New Criticism.[4] Overall, though, the dominant line of practice aimed at producing "readings" or interpretations of literature rather than filling in pieces of historical background. In a sense, criticism subsumed the task of scholarship: A literary scholar would produce new knowledge by producing new readings, and literary history, while still continuing, became a minor key in the discipline. In an influential essay of the time, the poet and critic Randall Jarrell deemed it "The Age of Criticism."

Along with that transformation, another notable change was a reorientation toward more modern objects of study. The field had primarily been an antiquarian one, but through the 1950s, critics expanded it to discuss Romantic and other nineteenth-century British literature, modernism, and a fuller range of American literature. The New Critics often dealt with modern literature and were strongly influenced by T. S. Eliot, who won the Nobel Prize in 1948. While sometimes opposed to the New Critics in emphasizing social and political issues, the New York Intellectuals, such as Lionel Trilling, also looked especially to modern literature.[5] This modernization of the object of study marked a shift from being a historical discipline to a critical and interpretive one.

The period was rich in literary commentary and debate—there was a wave of midcentury textbooks announcing the flourishing of American criticism, such as Zabel's *Literary Opinion in America*—but the evolution of the discipline was prompted not only by ideas; it was also spurred by changes in American higher education. The massive expansion of the American university and the dramatic increase of the student population after World War II created the conditions for the reorientation of scholarly work. As Gerald Graff shows in his classic account of the discipline, *Professing Literature: An Institutional History,* criticism took center stage because it provided a ready pedagogical method for the many new students flooding colleges and universities, those with less preparation in history and languages. It also provided a way for them to gain interpretive tools in an increasingly complex modern world rather than to memorize historical details. Typically, histories of literature or criticism are cast as processions of styles or ideas, but they are also responses to their social and institutional conditions.

By the 1960s, however, many raised reservations about criticism. Even Ransom complained that a good deal of it was shallow and doctrinal, the "merest exercises with words" (qtd. in Janssen 175). Others called for the social relevance of literary studies, finding most criticism, in centering on literary features, too removed from the world and in centering on highbrow texts, too elitist. Subsequently, the movements of the 1960s and 1970s in feminism and in civil rights made inroads into academic programs and inspired important wings of criticism and theory arising in the 1970s and 1980s. At the same time, a new wave of thought across the social sciences and philosophy, particularly continental philosophy, proposed sweeping changes to the way that scholars considered language, humanism, culture, society, and institutions. The wave that impacted American criticism was sometimes called French theory, as much of it came from French thinkers such as Claude Lévi-Strauss in anthropology, Jacques Lacan in psychoanalysis, Michel Foucault in social theory, Jacques Derrida in philosophy, and Roland Barthes in literary and cultural studies.[6] They became touchstones for the Age of Theory.

## II. The Age of Theory

### *i. The Discovery of Difference*

Initially, French theory aimed to create a new set of "human sciences," emulating the rigor of the harder social sciences. In particular, it looked to linguistics as a model, applying it to culture and society as well as to literature. While a critic might perform a reading of one poem, theory aimed to tell about the structure of literature overall just as linguistics might tell you the structure of language. For instance, the narrative theorist Tzvetan Todorov (who had been Barthes's student) argued in "Structural Analysis of Narrative" that "a New Critic . . . will have no goal other than an understanding of the work itself; the result of his efforts will be a paraphrase of the work" (70). Instead, he proposes to ascertain the pattern of plots in a wide breadth of narratives, which will yield a theory of narrative rather than an individual reading, similar to the way that a physicist would adduce a theory of gravity rather than describe one falling object. This effort to discern the underlying structure explains why it was called structuralism, and it fortified critical activity to conduct a more ambitious academic research program.

Linguistics was an apt model because it was a human science —defining a human activity rather than physical phenomena—and might be applied to other aspects of culture and society. In psychoanalysis, for instance, Lacan declared that "the unconscious is structured like a language," and one might read the language of fashion or tribal cultures or gender or political ideology. Some dubbed the new stress on language "the linguistic turn," and a main reference point for French theory was Ferdinand de Saussure, a founder of modern linguistics. Saussure had been active during the early part of the twentieth century, but his work was not widely known until the 1960s when it was translated. (Part of the story of criticism and theory is not only new work but the new use of older work.) Saussure's theory of language held that meaning is produced in a system of signs and that they gain significance not from positive correspondences but from negative differences. We tend to assume there is a necessary connection between a word and a thing or, more technically in Saussure's schema, a signifier and a signified—the words *ruff, ruff* presumably mirror how a dog barks. However, different languages use very different words for the same thing—*ouah, ouah* are words for a bark in French, *meong, meong* in Korean, and *gav, gav* in Russian. Thus, given the great diversity of languages, the connection between word and thing is not a necessary or inevitable one but arbitrary. We make meaning through negation, understanding words by their difference in their system; we understand *dog* refers to a dog because it is not *dig* or *dag*. Signifiers gain meaning by their difference from other signifiers.

Literary and cultural theory took as one of its main postulates this emphasis on difference, extending it to culture overall. In a sense, it fostered a theory of cultural relativity: if meaning was relational rather than absolute, then we only assign value through relative judgments rather than universal ones. Thus, we cannot declare an absolute value to a literary work or cultural practice, as it can only be understood in relation to other works or cultures in a system of differences. Furthermore, the differences tend to operate in binaries or oppositional pairs. That applies to concepts of measure like big or small—they are complementary antitheses, one the negation of the other, and they only have meaning relative to something else. A dog is small compared to a human but big compared to a chipmunk. It also applies to cultural concepts, like the fundamental distinction between nature and culture. We understand culture because it is not part of nature.

By the late 1960s, a critique from Jacques Derrida rechanneled the course of French theory, as he argued that binaries finally break down, a process that he famously named deconstruction, precipitating "poststructuralism." In *Of Grammatology* and other early works, Derrida critiqued Lévi-Strauss's anthropology, which held that every culture defines itself through its difference from nature. Derrida argued that while such binary oppositions might generate meaning, they finally deconstruct: the natural bleeds over to what we think of as cultural and vice versa. A dirt road might suggest a natural rather than city setting, but in a different frame, it is an artifice of culture, and in fact, in a forest given to logging, it might signal high-tech industry. Moreover, Derrida holds that binaries encode a hierarchy of values, so one term is privileged over the other and at the expense of the other. Thus, we not only distinguish culture and nature from one another but tend to value culture above nature. Or in literature, literary over popular fiction. Or in society, the masculine over the feminine. Or in civilizations, the center over the periphery. Derrida focused on the history of philosophy, but he often discussed literary examples, and his mode of critique—emphasizing the way meaning is built through a chain of signifiers and finally indeterminate—became a touchstone for literary scholars.

Derrida, of course, represented only one wing of theory, but he exemplified the tendency of theorists to question standard assumptions not only about literary works but about language, interpretation, knowledge, society, and institutions. That tendency, for example, influenced thinking about gender. A common assumption is that it is a natural category, determined biologically, but feminist theory emphasized how it is cultural and relational, constructed through the binary opposition of masculine and feminine. That opposition usually accords the masculine a higher value, placing the feminine in an inferior position (for instance, in the US, women get paid significantly less than men for the same work). The critique of gender and accentuation of its construction formed a major plank in feminist criticism, as well as subsequent versions of gay, lesbian, queer, and trans theory. The theoretical emphasis on difference led to a critique of social differences, viewing much of our thinking on race, gender, sexuality, and ethnicity not as natural givens but as cultural constructions. A major consequence of the theory of difference has been to see our social categories as cultural constructions.

An important institutional factor in the rise of theory was the further development of American higher education, notably the dramatic enhancement of research. Research had been a component of the previous formation of the university, but during the 1960s and 1970s, it moved front and center. By about 1970, as the sociologists Jencks and Riesman reported in *The Academic Revolution*, American universities shifted to stress research over teaching, graduate education over undergraduate, and professional interests over campus ones. In literary studies alone, the number of PhDs in English increased from about 400 in 1960 to 1,100 in 1970.[7] While not all faculty members conduct significant research, and the American system encompasses a range of institutions, research became the primary rationale of scholarly training and work, and theory provided a research agenda for English studies. It furnished "tools" or templates to produce a presumably more advanced knowledge of literary and cultural works beyond the pedagogical task of explicating a particular work.

A conjoined factor was the investment in and flourishing of foreign languages. Indeed, much continental theory first came through departments of French, German, Slavic, and comparative literature. Those disciplines saw their heyday, experiencing unprecedented financial support and prestige as part of the expansion of the place of the US in the world. The more idealistic side of American policy in the period after World War II, as the US became a superpower, aimed for an understanding of other cultures, although the less idealistic side aimed to counter the Soviet Union in the long Cold War.[8] The space race with the Soviet Union after it had launched Sputnik, the first rocket into space, prompted the National Defense Education Act of 1958, which was enhanced in 1965 and several times thereafter, and fertilized the ground for the developments of the 1970s and 1980s (see Lewontin). However revolutionary its claims, the profusion of theory occurred under the auspices of the expansion of the American footprint on the globe.

## *ii. The Schools of Theory*

From the late 1960s through the 1980s, theory aligned in six or so schools or approaches, as mentioned above, usually including formalism or structuralism, deconstruction, Marxism, feminism, psychoanalysis, and reader response. By the late 1980s and into the 1990s, they were followed by offshoots such as the new historicism, gay and lesbian criticism, and postcolonial theory. Most literary scholars affiliated with one or another approach, often inciting turf wars between camps. For example, Marxist critics charged deconstructive critics with blindness to social concerns, whereas deconstructive critics held that one had to understand the complexities of language before anything else, and Marxist critics were subject to mystification. That gradually changed as subsequent scholars tended to assimilate multiple approaches.

To look at each in turn:

**Formalism** generally focuses on literary features, patterns, or types. Sometimes the New Criticism was inducted into the menu of theory retroactively as a kind of formalism, although in its own time, it was primarily a practical criticism, aimed at prompting readings of particular texts rather than an overarching theory. One of the main New Critics, Cleanth Brooks, for instance, produces readings of poems from John Donne to T. S. Eliot in his landmark book *The Well-Wrought Urn.* His title captures the formalist idea: the unified composition of a literary work.

**Structuralism** likewise tends to focus on literary features and sometimes was considered a fortified formalism, but it aimed to describe literature systematically, for instance, in narrative theory adducing the set of fundamental plot types. In the hands of the narratologist Tzvetan Todorov, it aimed for a "poetics" or abstract understanding of the forms of literature. After a brief flourishing, it largely ceded by the 1980s, as critics focused more on the difficulties of language and indeterminacy of meaning—for instance, after early efforts to ascertain structure, Barthes moved to the unruly multiplicity of meaning in his book *S/Z.*

**Deconstruction** tends to emphasize language and the slippage of definite meaning. Derrida underscored the "free play of the signifier," although in the hands of Paul de Man, arguably the most influential American theorist of the late 1970s and 1980s, it emphasized how texts resist interpretation to finally result in indeterminacy. In his book *Allegories of Reading*, de Man found that literary texts foreground the problems of language, and critics after him were much more conscious of the uncertainty involved in critical understanding. One can see the residual influence of deconstruction in, for instance, queer theory, which foregrounds the slippage and lack of determinacy of sexual identities.

**Reader response** criticism and theory explores the processes of reading, on one pole the phenomenological act of reading and on the other the historical accumulation of readings of literary works. Often, reader response is misunderstood as simply indicating that every reader has his or her individual impression, but it looks at interpretation more rigorously, in the tradition of hermeneutics (see Holub). Like deconstruction, it underscores the complexity of interpretation, but it does not find it to result in a crisis of uncertainty, instead offering a middle-ground position. In the work of Wolfgang Iser, for example, it pragmatically looks at the way that readers fill in gaps, similar to the way a performance of a play actualizes a script. The script is neither uncertain nor subjective, although each performance is an interpretation. In contrast, reception theory turns to another facet of reading, the actual history of interpretations of literary works rather than a particular experience. It holds that we never see works in and of themselves, as a formalist might claim, but always through the historical filter of criticism and ideas of a time, governing our expectations of works. Those expectations in turn determine whether we find particular works conventional, shocking, or innovative and in turn condition how we interpret them.

**Psychoanalysis** tends to focus on the construction of subjectivity in texts. Psychoanalysis has had a long history in criticism from early twentieth-century readings of phallic symbols or the Oedipal complex in texts. For instance, one early reading of *Hamlet* simply psychoanalyzed the character; in contrast, contemporary psychoanalysis, inspired by Jacques Lacan, looks in more complicated terms at how language creates our subjectivity and how it expresses desire.

**Feminism** turns the attention of criticism toward gender and sexuality. In US criticism, feminism first focused on the skewed portrait of women in literature, as well as argued for more attention to women authors in the canon, recovering many that were largely forgotten, in a wave of scholarly works in the 1970s like Elaine Showalter's *A Literature of Their Own*. In the 1980s, the debate shifted to "French feminism" and a more theoretical questioning of the stable category of woman. In addition, some pointed to the limitations of feminism, as the work of the 1970s tended to take the standpoint of majority culture, of white, middle-class women, and argued for lesbian feminist criticism, black feminist criticism, and other minority identities.

**Marxism** tends to look at the ways that texts express or reproduce ideology. Early Marxism, under the auspices of Soviet aesthetics, tended toward a "reflectionist" theory—that is, finding that artworks directly reflect their society—whereas more contemporary versions look at the way that they might be influenced by ideology, create ideology, and express ideological contradictions. Since the 1970s, the most influential theorist advocating Marxism in literary studies has been Fredric Jameson, whose *The Political Unconscious: Narrative as a Socially Symbolic Act* teased out the "ideology of form" of literary works. Jameson declared in that book that we should "always historicize," which has had a great deal of influence, with many looking at the social and historical implications of literature, especially at the force of capitalism and its expression in literary works.

While the schools of theory usually aimed to stake out distinctive positions, there were some alliances among schools. For example, psychoanalysis might lead to a narrow reading of the language of desire in a text, but it also might have political consequences for feminism, as in Laura Mulvey's "Visual Pleasure and Narrative Cinema," which famously showed how film typically centers on "the male gaze" with the camera dwelling on women and women's bodies. Her reading of the psychic assumptions of film carried an influential social critique—our culture internalizes the perspective of men, as even women might see themselves in that lens. In a different mode, Gayatri Spivak developed a fusion of deconstructive, Marxist, and feminist approaches, helping to develop postcolonial studies, although she was unusual in doing that at the time.

By the late 1980s and early 1990s, several new initiatives emerged, notably the new historicism, gay and lesbian studies, and postcolonial theory. In addition, theory developed around race studies, notably in the US from African American studies. They drew on previous theory but did not adhere as strictly to a school; for example, the new historicism, while beckoning a renewal of scholarship and literary history, adopted a poststructural tenet of textuality, seeing history as a text that we construct rather than a set of facts we can recover. Unlike previous literary historians, the new historicists did not aim to establish direct historical causality, but, drawing on Michel Foucault's analysis of discourse, they speculated on the general ideology that works responded to and expressed. For example, in a major book by Stephen Greenblatt, *Shakespearean Negotiations*, he recounts the trial of a hermaphrodite in France around Shakespeare's time, which suggests the fluid character of gender in the discourse of the time. Greenblatt does not establish a direct historical connection—the trial was remote and almost certainly not known to Shakespeare—but rather uses the anecdote to illuminate the play *Twelfth Night*. The new historicism represents the fusion of historical scholarship with poststructural theoretical notions of discourse.

By the late 1980s, those studying gender pointed out the limitations and binary notions of gender and sexuality in much feminism. They applied a deconstructive critique to such categories, developing gay and lesbian criticism and theory, notably in the work of Eve Kosofsky Sedgwick, who was a one-time student of de Man's. Through the 1990s, theorists like Sedgwick and Butler turned to the more indeterminate category of queer theory. For instance, Sedgwick pointed out that there are a great variety of practices among even presumably heterosexual couples, and Butler's landmark book, *Gender Trouble*, shows how gender is not a natural or even a durable construction but is, in fact, a temporal performance. Queer theory carries a tacit political critique:

binary categories are used to constrain, if not ostracize, those who practice alternative sexualities, and we should recognize the undecidability of gender and sexuality.

Also pointing to the way that dominant culture excluded others, during the 1970s and 1980s, scholars pointed out the absence of attention to African Americans in the canon and its whiteness. Through the 1980s, critics like Henry Louis Gates Jr. foregrounded "Race, Writing, and Difference," in the title of an influential collection organized by Gates, and over the next decade, critics developed various perspectives on race and ethnicity, such as Chicano and Hispanic American criticism and theory, Asian American, and more specific denominators, and ethnicities like Italian American studies. The focus on identity and its variants, which deconstruct conventional biases about race, gender, ethnicity, sexuality, and abledness, came to influence criticism over the next two decades.

In the intersection between race studies, Marxian-inflected criticism of imperialism, and deconstruction, postcolonial theory was one of the most prominent avenues of theory to emerge in the 1980s and early 1990s. From race studies, it emphasized the negative cast projected on the racial or ethnic other, especially in the context of the nation, and from Marxism it looked to the historical and political effects of imperialism. While Marxism often set itself against deconstruction, postcolonial theory absorbed the critique of the hierarchy of terms like *center* and *margin*, or *citizen* and *other*, breaking down such oppositions. Edward Said helped forge the field in his pathbreaking book *Orientalism* and foregrounded the effects of imperialism in *Culture and Imperialism*. Although he criticized the excessive preoccupation of deconstruction with language, his critique of orientalism drew on the critique of oppositions like "margin" and "center," or for him the orient and the occident, and in general postcolonial critics explained how the center and margin are in fact interdependent, with "the other" a projection of the center and the center often incorporating the marginal (think of food, for example).

If Paul de Man was the most prominent critic on the American scene from the mid-1970s through the 1980s, promoting deconstruction and its focus on language and the literary over history and social context, then Said was probably the most prominent critic from the 1980s through around 2000, advocating a more "worldly" criticism and looking at literature as an expression of culture and politics.[9] Trained at Harvard as a comparative literature scholar a short time after de Man, Said was grounded in the literary tradition and frequently wrote about canonical literary texts, but his work, particularly from *Orientalism* onward, embedded them in their cultural, institutional, and political contexts. In addition, he was a harbinger of the model of the public intellectual, often appearing in mainstream media sources (for instance, writing for *The Nation* and appearing regularly on television news shows like *Nightline*, especially commenting on the politics of the Middle East). That model gained traction through the 1990s in answer to complaints about the obscurity of theory. De Man carried out the charge to look at the special qualities of language and the literary, whereas Said augured the turn of English studies to the broader domains of culture and politics.

## III. The Age of Cultural Studies

### *i. The Expansion of Theory*

By the 1990s, theory had become mainstream, not only in academe but in popular culture—there was even an alternative band that named itself Deconstruction, with a self-titled debut album in 1994. In turn, some questioned its new dominance. Some reacted against the professionalization that theory signaled and advocated for a more personal connection to literature, calling for "personal" or "autobiographical criticism" (see N. Miller). Some, like Stanley Fish, argued that theory had "no consequences" and was a professional game. Yet others complained of "Theory's Empire" (see Patai) at the expense of literature itself. Theory went from being a disruptive new practice to an expected mode of proceeding, one that has continued to the present.

Indeed, if you read contemporary criticism or scholarship, you can usually see the explicit use of theory in it. It probably cites theorists that it aligns itself with, as well as those it questions or opposes. It might claim to make an "intervention" in theoretical debates of its moment. However, a notable difference from the 1970s is that theory has become less singular or wedded to a specific school or method, combining with other approaches to explore an area or subfield of study. Since the 1990s, the general direction has shifted from making large claims about language, interpretation, or society overall to investigating new fields or subfields of culture. The fields of study have expanded from conventional literary periods to the varieties of culture. Many of them are based on the permutations of identity, some on media, some on theoretical focuses like affect, and some social concerns like the environment. To take one example, arguments about gender have expanded from the binary frame of masculine and feminine to the diversity of genders and sexualities in queer theory, masculinity studies, trans theory, and other body studies.

The multiplication of new scholarly initiatives has generally been construed under the wide umbrella of cultural studies, and some see the turn toward cultural studies as a decisive break akin to the theory revolution. In the title of a book by Anthony Easthope, it marks a paradigm shift from "literary into cultural studies." However, theory remains the prime motor for scholarly work, and by and large English and foreign language departments remain its home base and proceed according to the residual structure of courses in literary fields and periods with faculty accredited to teach them, adding new areas like media or digital culture. In other words, while it marks a change, it represents an expansion, continuing the research program of theory, rather than a decisive rupture.

Theory has not been superseded but, in fact, catalyzed the development of these fields, generating ways to open new areas that have arisen through the 1990s and 2000s. This has led a leading historian of modern criticism, Vincent Leitch, to argue that rather than the wane or exhaustion of theory that some have asserted, we have seen a "theory renaissance," and he lists ninety active areas in current literary studies organized around twelve nodes. If one noted microfields and identities, there could be many more. To organize the main lines of cultural studies, I would mark out five general categories: some organize around the body and identity with theories about genders and sexualities and also new fields like disability studies and age studies. Some organize around race and region, catalyzed by postcolonial theory toward broad initiatives like transatlantic studies, Pacific Rim studies, and globalization, and others in more narrowly specified pursuits, like Caribbean or Haitian studies, Native American and other indigenous studies, and the many permutations thereof.

A third cluster organizes around media, which first centered on film studies but has expanded, looking back at book history and print culture and forward to sound theory, visual culture, new media, and digital culture, and which has spawned areas like celebrity studies. A fourth cluster revolves around theoretical concepts like affect, which draws on psychoanalytic theory but also looks to alternatives like cognitive theory and has led to work in traditional fields like aesthetics and more socially directed pursuits like trauma studies. A fifth cluster turns toward social and political issues like ecocriticism, animal studies, cosmopolitanism, and neoliberalism.

In short, English studies has become a meeting place of many pursuits. Since the first wave of theory, the aim has morphed from building a core of "human sciences" to exploring diverse fields of "studies." In some sense, the impetus of theory toward difference has led to the multiplication of studies and to their organization under the wide rubric of culture rather than the narrow and exclusive notion of literature. One consequence of poststructural critiques of hierarchal categories is to see literature simply as one element of culture among others rather than a privileged one, and English studies widened to literary *and* cultural studies. In some conservative complaints about the advent of cultural studies, it is taken to mean giving up the study of literature to look at vulgar popular culture. But in a more neutral view, what has happened is a general expansion, retaining the base of literary fields but assimilating additional ones, driven by the logic of innovation of programs of research.

A telling register of the change in criticism and theory is the orientation of the textbooks in it. While the rise of theory saw a wave of general theory anthologies designating the main schools, since around 2000 the main text has shifted to the reader, the anthology of work in a specific field or area of study. They were pioneered with *The New Historicism Reader*; *The Gay and Lesbian Studies Reader*; *The Postcolonial Studies Reader*; and *African American Literary Theory: A Reader*. There followed a flood of volumes marking specified fields or subfields, such as *The*

*Ecocriticism Reader*; *The Disability Studies Reader*; *Science Studies Reader*; *The Visual Culture Reader*; *The Masculinity Studies Reader*; *The Chicana/o Cultural Studies Reader*; *The Transgender Studies Reader*; *The Affect Theory Reader*; and *Defining Digital Humanities: A Reader*. In each field or on each topic, there are often several competing readers as well as hybrids among them, such as *Queer Feminist Science Studies: A Reader*, and even more specified fields, such as *Critical Surf Studies Reader*.

One way to explain this expansion is on the model of fractals. English studies has never been a narrowly unified discipline, as it has incorporated diverse pursuits since its inception. In his book *Chaos of Disciplines*, Andrew Abbott, a leading sociologist of professions, has observed that academic disciplines in the modern university tend to accumulate more fields or subfields over time. Borrowing the physical model of fractal behavior from chaos theory, he speculates that disciplines spin off new fields or subfields that operate similarly to the larger field. They develop their own protocols, terms, theory, and touchstone theorists, similar to the way that a small rivulet exhibits the same bends, pools, and runs as a large river. Furthermore, instead of supplanting older areas of study or different theories, disciplines tend to agglomerate them, "becom[ing] a discipline of many topics—always acquiring them, seldom losing them" (*Chaos* 6). While Abbott's focus is sociology, the same framework applies to English, as it has absorbed new approaches, adding them without jettisoning others. Hence, we might have high theory along with literary history, media studies with close reading of classic literature, Asian American studies with medieval British literature, digital data with creative writing, object-oriented ontology with composition studies, the new formalism with political critique of neoliberalism, and so on.

If anything, this process exhibits the intensification of the research protocol, producing ever new methods, fields, and specializations. It is part of the tendency of institutionalization: like corporations, disciplines seem driven to grow or die. On the one hand, it presents the positive intellectual potential of producing new knowledge, exploring new domains, inventing new critical lenses, opening our thought to new critical insights. On the other hand, particularly if one takes the critical edge of theory to question our tacit assumptions, it also seems to follow the logic of contemporary capitalist business corporations, expanding by perpetually developing new products and inciting the desire for them, to perpetuate the system of power already in place. This less positive prospect has been rarely examined, even in theory that targets neoliberal capitalism. One new field that has started to investigate the influence of capitalist practices in higher education is critical university studies—that influence comes through often harmful but highly profitable policies and practices such as student debt, as well as the adoption of corporate business principles to university administration and labor, rather than grounding it in principles of the public good without private profit (see Williams, "Need"). Still, we should not lose sight of the potential of higher education or other forms of public education to foster critical investigation, thought, and action. Given that more than three-quarters of young Americans attend higher education at some point, the university is not an ivory tower but in the thick of American cultural and political life, and one strength of English studies is its disposition toward the critical and theoretical examination of institutions as well as texts and ideas.

That goes some way toward explaining the institutional logic of the development of cultural studies. Another factor that bears mention is the more general context of American cultural politics. In some ways, the move toward cultural studies carries out the American tenet of pluralism and diversity, emblematic of a country built from the immigration of many peoples and creeds rather than from a single, original core. That view, however, has enjoined a great deal of public controversy, erupting in the culture wars during the late 1980s and early 1990s and continuing in various ways since. At their heart, the culture wars represent a struggle over views of difference. The progressive view is to celebrate cultural differences and see the resulting multiculturalism as a virtue of the US experiment. In contrast, the conservative view is to see multiculturalism as a breakdown in attaining a common culture. Cultural studies generally assumes that presenting the panorama of cultures without privileging a particular one promotes the aim of democracy. The counter view holds that multiculturalism fractures culture to a cacophony of identities and, in its relativism, abandons the edifying value of studying great literature. The tension between these two views still looms over English studies.

## *ii. The New Humanities*

Since around 2010, one striking new direction has been the development of work linking English studies with major social or conceptual topics like the environment or technology. Rather than cultural "studies," they often take the suffix "humanities" in amalgams such as the digital humanities, the environmental humanities, the energy humanities, the global humanities, the medical humanities, and the public humanities. Cultural studies has tended to draw on sibling disciplines in the humanities like history, art history, and film studies, or cousin disciplines in the social sciences like anthropology and sociology, whereas the new humanities tend to link with STEM fields in the sciences as well as applied or practical disciplines like engineering, computing, statistics, and public policy or management. They bring humanist frameworks to bear on technical or practical fields like medicine, as well as bring those fields into English studies.

Perhaps the most prominent cluster has organized around the digital humanities, adopting methods of quantification from statistics and computing. Franco Moretti has been a leading figure among literary scholars in this impetus, proposing "distant reading" to adduce general patterns through quantitative means. Typical literary methods, he argues, give an extraordinarily limited picture of the history of literature at any given time, as they deal with a small canon examined in the micro-detail of "close reading." The digital humanities looks instead at the macro-picture: Moretti, for example, aims for a way to discern the evolution of genres of the novel over a long period of time, similar to the way a biologist might look at the evolution of trees. The interest of the biologist is not the shape or beauty of a particular tree, but the qualities of trees in general and the arc of their evolution.

While the digital humanities is theoretical—it aims to abstract hypotheses from large bodies of data—it suggests a break from previous theory and cultural studies. It takes an empirical basis, like a life science, over a hermeneutic basis, dwelling on the complex nature of interpretation. Notably, it departs from the epistemological and interpretive preoccupations of French theory, as well as its focus on societal critique. It feeds into a larger movement toward what Stephen Best and Sharon Marcus have named "surface reading," in which they include formalist approaches as well as digital ones. Best and Marcus criticize the tendency of previous theorists for their overreach in claiming an explicit political effect for scholarly work and advise more narrowly descriptive techniques. In addition, they suggest that the moment of theory was generational, one that is now passing, with these new approaches superseding it.

Another prominent cluster has organized around the environment and the harmful effects of capitalism. Emphasizing literary and other modes of representation, the environmental humanities links especially with the life sciences, particularly about global climate change, and studies of the Anthropocene, the period since humans altered the condition of the earth. It underscores not only the devastation of climate change but the political consequences of it, both for those countries that use the most resources and those that are exploited. Unlike the digital humanities, this cluster tends to follow the political impulse of cultural studies. Works like Rob Nixon's *Slow Violence and Environmentalism of the Poor* expose the damaging effects of climate change particularly on the poor and the most vulnerable, alongside other writers' efforts to bring such problems to social justice. A related branch of the environmental humanities concentrates on resources like oil and more specifically concentrates on the energy humanities, and another underscores the patterns of migration of people and the networks through which goods are manufactured and distributed around the world, constituting the world of global humanities. In exposing the migration of waste as well as productive resources, they intertwine with the environmental humanities.

More specifically focused on an institution, the medical or health humanities forge a link with perhaps the major social institution of contemporary society, bringing humanistic perspectives to medicine and showing their practical use. The medical humanities has taken a role in healthcare training, offering doctors and nurses ways of knowing other than purely scientific ones, for instance in developing "narrative medicine," examining stories of cases and how patients might recount their issues, which add a unique mode of information to medical understanding beyond lab tests and numbers on a medical chart. There also has been a similar impetus in bringing humanistic perspectives to law, in a cluster sometimes called law and the humanities or the legal humanities.

A more internal impetus within the humanities has been an effort to bring its work to a wider public, fostering "the public humanities." From the side of the humanities, it aims to make academic work more accessible and useful to a general public in publishing on literary or cultural matters in mainstream magazines or newspapers or to more specific publics, for instance to public policy groups or community organizations. In addition to promoting academic work outside academic quadrants, another side of the public humanities prompts those in academe to move outward, working with community organizations particularly in the nonprofit world, for instance in museums or art groups or in social services, with many students doing internships or "service learning," for example, in programs tutoring in an impoverished area. The public humanities tacitly works to redress the distance that theory or simply advanced research has created between academic practice and the wider public, so in some ways it represents a withdrawal from theory—not necessarily renouncing it, but displacing it from its dominant position and recasting the task of literary studies.

These new configurations of the humanities embrace the prospect of interdisciplinarity, crossing the divides between disciplines and providing a more holistic look at a problem or area such as the environment. They bring humanistic knowledge to other fields, and they bring other knowledges to English. On the one hand, they seem to carry out an altruistic vision of academic work unconstrained by traditional institutional boundaries and enjoin flexible, pragmatic uses of theoretical work. On the other hand, however, in their actual implementation, they often represent the marginalization of English and other classic disciplines in the humanities, subordinating them to business and other applied disciplines, and they neutralize the critical charge of theory. They are typically celebrated as collaborative, but the key question is what end do these partnerships serve? In the Latin phrase, *Qui bono?* Who benefits? And who controls them?

Sometimes practical disciplines operate less for the sake of exploring knowledge and more to serve mercantile ventures that benefit private stakeholders rather than intellectual or public interests. As Rob Nixon remarks of the environmental humanities, "there is a risk of humanities scholars entering into partnerships uncritically, in ways that become complicit with the neoliberal agendas of universities rebranding themselves as 'sustainable'" (175). And as Jonathan Kramnick argues in "The Interdisciplinary Delusion," disciplines provide an organizational structure to protect pursuits and knowledges for the sake of human understanding, particularly in a time when it seems that business pursuits assume all priority. Kramnick neatly distinguishes the two goals of business and academic work: corporations aim "to maximize private profit" whereas universities seek to "explain the world," and we need different disciplines to explain different facets of the world.

Perhaps the major institutional factor confronting English studies and those in the humanities over the past twenty years has been the shrinking of support. Though it is hard to assess what effect this has had on scholarship, criticism, and theory, it surely shapes the possibilities of criticism just as previous institutional conditions molded the field of practice. Sometimes it seems as if ideas proceed by their own logic or force, but criticism has developed in response to its material conditions. If the previous era of academic expansion bolstered English studies and especially spurred research, the current decline of support has affected the possibilities for both majors and faculty. Over the past decade, English majors have decreased—not necessarily because of lack of interest but because of the stress on pursuing immediately marketable, business-oriented degrees, even though historically English majors have done well over the long-term arc of their careers. For faculty, a majority of positions have been reconfigured from fully fledged professorial positions that encourage research to adjunct, part-time, or impermanent positions, largely to teach basic writing or other service courses. This has had consequences for research: for those with research-oriented positions, it probably intensifies the pressure on research, particularly the pressure to do research that aims to appeal to the market rather than independent intellectual concerns. For the majority with more precarious positions, it reconfigures faculty in English studies as teachers serving the new university hierarchy of values rather than as equal participants in the exploration of knowledge. How this will tone the future of critical theory and cultural studies is uncertain, but the institutional situation is bound to alter the practices in the discipline.

## Notes

1. Theory first gained traction in foreign language or comparative literature departments, particularly at major universities like Yale, Johns Hopkins, and Columbia, and then spread through English studies. In an interview, the feminist critic Jane Gallop recounts how she learned about the new theory during the 1970s while a student in Romance studies at Cornell, subsequently transitioning into English in the late 1980s. She remarks that, "The reason I wanted to get out of French and into English was not because I wanted to work on English literature, but because I wanted a bigger audience and bigger world in which to read and write" (90).

2. See my history of "The Rise of the Theory Journal" as well as my more general account of anthologies and other texts in "The Book History of Theory."

3. "Critical theory" was also an impetus that a group of German critics, organized around the Frankfurt Institute for Social Research and loosely Marxist, called their activity, but the Frankfurt school had its greatest influence in social theory and relatively little application in literary studies.

4. See Leitch for a full account of the various schools and progress of criticism across the century.

5. See Trilling's "On the Teaching of Modern Literature"; likewise, Irving Howe, a major New York Intellectual, defined "the idea of the modern" in a volume so titled.

6. Initially "French theory" was sometimes an aspersion, noting its foreign imposition into American criticism, but by about 2010, it became

accepted as a neutral description, for instance in Cusset's *French Theory*. Probably the better survey, however, is Dosse, *History of Structuralism*.

7. H 766–87, Number of Doctorates, by Field: 1920–1970. Washington, DC: US Bureau of the Census.

8. Most notably, the Truman Commission Report, more formally known as *Higher Education for American Democracy: A Report of the President's Commission on Higher Education*, 6 vols. (New York: Harper, 1947), which set the direction of policy in the coming years, called for improving education across the US. In particular, it called for free public higher education to augment equality. In addition, it called for "an active appreciation of different cultures and other peoples" (Vol. 1, 14) and "a sympathetic understanding of . . . eastern Europe, Asia, Africa, South America, and the islands of the sea" (17) to encourage Americans to "move from the provincial and insular mind to the international mind" (15). To understand other cultures, policy especially bolstered foreign language training and departments; see Joseph Axelrod and Donald M. Bigelow, *Resources for Language and Area Studies: A Report on an Inventory of the Language and Area Centers Supported by the National Defense Education Act of 1958* (Washington, DC: American Council on Education, 1962).

9. De Man declared that the task of criticism was to look at the "bafflement" of language and he dismissed those who think of "the teaching of literature as a substitute for the teaching of theology, ethics, psychology, or intellectual history" (24). In *The World, the Text, and the Critic*, Said tacitly criticizes de Man's position: "literary theory has for the most part isolated textuality from the circumstances, the events, the physical that made it possible and render it intelligible as the result of human work," and declared that "My position is that texts are worldly . . . part of the social world . . . and of course the historical moments in which they are located and interpreted" (4).

## Works Cited

Abbott, Andrew. *Chaos of Disciplines*. U of Chicago P, 2001.

Abelove, Henry, Michèle Aina Barale, and David M. Halperin, editors. *The Lesbian and Gay Studies Reader*. Routledge, 1993.

Abrams, M. H. "A Life in Criticism: An Interview with M. H. Abrams." With Jeffrey J. Williams. *Minnesota Review*, vol. 69, 2007, pp. 71–93.

Adams, Hazard, and Leroy Searle, editors. *Critical Theory since 1965.* U of Florida P, 1986.

Ashcroft, Bill, Gareth Griffiths, and Helen Tiffin, editors. *The Post-Colonial Studies Reader.* Routledge, 1995.

Barthes, Roland. *S/Z.* 1970. Translated by Richard Miller. Hill and Wang, 1975.

Bate, W. Jackson. "The Crisis in English Studies." *Harvard Magazine,* Sept.–Oct. 1982, pp. 46–53.

Best, Stephen, and Sharon Marcus. "Surface Reading: An Introduction." *Representations*, vol. 108, no. 1, 2009, pp. 1–21.

Brandt, H. C. G. "How Far Should Our Teaching and Text-books Have a Scientific Basis?" *The Origins of Literary Study in America: A Documentary Anthology*, edited by Gerald Graff and Michael Warner, Routledge, 1989, pp. 22–33.

Brooks, Cleanth. *The Well-Wrought Urn: Studies in the Structure of Poetry.* 1947. Harcourt Brace, 1956.

Butler, Judith. *Gender Trouble: Feminism and the Subversion of Identity.* Routledge, 1990.

Crane, R. S. "Criticism as Inquiry; or, the Perils of the 'High Priori' Road." 1957. *The Idea of the Humanities and Other Essays Critical and Historical Vol.* 2. U of Chicago P, 1967, pp. 25–44.

———. "History versus Criticism in the Study of Literature." 1935. *The Idea of the Humanities and Other Essays Critical and Historical Vol.* 2. U of Chicago P, 1967, pp. 3–24.

Cusset, François. *French Theory: How Foucault, Derrida, Deleuze, & Co. Transformed the Intellectual Life of the United States.* Translated by Jeff Fort, U of Minnesota P, 2008.

De Man, Paul. *Allegories of Reading: Figural Language in Rousseau, Nietzsche, Rilke, and Proust.* Yale UP, 1979.

———. *The Resistance to Theory.* U of Minnesota P, 1986.

Derrida, Jacques. *Of Grammatology.* 1967. Translated by Gayatri Chakravorty Spivak. Johns Hopkins UP, 1976.

Dosse, François. *History of Structuralism.* 2 vols. Translated by Deborah Glassman. U of Minnesota P, 1998.

Easthope, Anthony. *Literary into Cultural Studies.* Routledge, 1991.

Gallop, Jane. "Sexual/Theoretical Politics: An Interview with Jane Gallop." With Jeffrey J. Williams. *Diacritics*, vol. 46, no. 3, 2018, pp. 80–98.

Gates, Henry Louis, Jr., editor. *"Race," Writing, and Difference.* U of Chicago P, 1986.

Graff, Gerald. *Professing Literature: An Institutional History.* U of Chicago P, 1987.

Greenblatt, Stephen. *Shakespearean Negotiations: The Circulation of Social Energy in Renaissance England.* U of California P, 1989.

Holub, Robert. "Reception Theory: School of Constance." *The Cambridge History of Literary Criticism, Vol. VIII: From Formalism to Poststructuralism.* Edited by Raman Selden. Cambridge UP, 1995, pp. 319–46.

Howe, Irving, editor. *The Idea of the Modern in Literature and the Arts.* Horizon Press, 1967.

Hyman, Stanley Edgar. *The Armed Vision: A Study in the Methods of Modern Literary Criticism.* Rev. ed., Vintage, 1955.

Iser, Wolfgang. "The Reading Process: A Phenomenological Approach." *The Implied Reader: Patterns of Communication in Prose Fiction from Bunyan to Beckett.* Johns Hopkins UP, 1974, pp. 274–94.

Jameson, Fredric. *The Political Unconscious: Narrative as a Socially Symbolic Act.* Cornell UP, 1981.

Janssen, Marian. *The Kenyon Review 1939–1970: A Critical History.* Louisiana State UP, 1990.

Jarrell, Randall. "The Age of Criticism." *Poetry and the Age.* Knopf, 1953, pp. 70–95.

Jencks, Christopher, and David Riesman. *The Academic Revolution.* Doubleday, 1968.

Knapp, Steven, and Walter Benn Michaels. "Against Theory." 1982. *Against Theory: Literary Studies and the New Pragmatism*, edited by W. J. T. Mitchell, U of Chicago P, 1985, pp. 11–30.

Kramnick, Jonathan. "The Interdisciplinary Delusion." *The Chronicle of Higher Education,* 11 Oct. 2018, https://www.chronicle.com/article/the-interdisciplinary-delusion.

Leitch, Vincent B. *American Literary Criticism since the 1930s*. 2nd ed. Routledge, 2009.

———. *Literary Criticism in the 21st Century: Theory Renaissance*. Bloomsbury Academic, 2014.

Lewontin, R. C. "The Cold War and the Transformation of the Academy." *Cold War & the University: Toward an Intellectual History of the Postwar Years*, edited by Noam Chomsky, et al. New Press, 1997, pp. 1–34.

Miller, J. Hillis. "Presidential Address 1986: The Triumph of Theory, the Resistance to Reading, and the Question of Material Base." *Theory Now and Then*. Duke UP, 1991, pp. 309–27.

Miller, Nancy K. *Getting Personal: Feminist Occasions and Other Autobiographical Acts*. Routledge, 1991.

Moretti, Franco. *Distant Reading*. Verso, 2013.

Mulvey, Laura. "Visual Pleasure and Narrative Cinema." *Screen*, vol. 16, no. 3, 1975, pp. 6–18.

Napier, Winston, editor. *African American Literary Theory: A Reader*. New York UP, 2000.

Nixon, Rob. *Slow Violence and the Environmentalism of the Poor*. Harvard UP, 2011.

———. "Criticism as a Kind of Nonfiction: An Interview with Rob Nixon." With Jeffrey J. Williams. *Iowa Review*, vol. 49, no. 2, 2019, pp. 173–92.

Norris, Frank. "The 'English Courses' of the University of California." 1896. *Novels and Essays*. Library of America, 1985, pp. 1109–11.

Patai, Daphne, and Will H. Corral, editors. *Theory's Empire: An Anthology of Dissent*. Columbia UP, 2005.

Ransom, John Crowe. "Criticism, Inc." *The World's Body*. Louisiana State UP, 1968, pp. 327–50.

Said, Edward W. *Culture and Imperialism*. Knopf, 1993.

———. *Orientalism*. Pantheon, 1978.

———. *The World, the Text, and the Critic*. Harvard UP, 1983.

Showalter, Elaine. *A Literature of Their Own: British Women Novelists from Brontë to Lessing*. Princeton UP, 1977.

Todorov, Tzvetan and Arnold Weinstein. "Structural Analysis of Narrative." *NOVEL: A Forum on Fiction*, vol. 3, no. 1, 1969, pp. 70–76.

Trilling, Lionel. "On the Teaching of Modern Literature." *Beyond Culture: Essays on Literature and Learning*. Viking, 1965, pp. 3–27.

Veeser, H. Aram, editor. *The New Historicism Reader*. Routledge, 1993.

Wellek, René. "Destroying Literary Studies." *New Criterion,* Dec. 1983, pp. 1–8.

Williams, Jeffrey J. "The Book History of Theory." *Symploke*, vol. 27, nos. 1–2, 2019, pp. 443–49.

———. "The Need for Critical University Studies." *A New Deal for the Humanities*, edited by Gordon Hutner and Feisal G. Mohammed. Rutgers UP, 2015, pp. 145–59.

———. "The Rise of the Theory Journal." *New Literary History*, vol. 40, no. 4, 2009, pp. 683–702.

Zabel, Morton Dauwen, editor. *Literary Opinion in America*. Rev. ed., Harper, 1951.

# *English Education*

TONYA B. PERRY
*University of Alabama at Birmingham*

"You don't live where I live," stated my eighth-grade student, Alvin. "I live in the city."

"You are right. I don't live here. Tell me more." The other students became engaged in the conversation. Other eighth graders started chiming in to educate me, their teacher, about the community.

Alvin led the discussion. "You want us to turn in these English worksheets, but when we leave school, we got things to do. We got to take care of our little brothers and sisters. We got things to do. We got to make it."

On the surface, it would appear that Alvin was saying, "Don't give us homework; we have other things to do." However, that was not the case. Alvin was asking, in his eighth-grade way, that I first understand who he was and what he had to offer. He was saying this: "Understand and appreciate me. Affirm who I am. Teach me, keeping in mind who I am as you teach me what else I need to be successful." He was asking me to examine my English teaching practice and frankly, my low, routine expectations. How would he ever use the basic English skills I dissected? How could he find enough relevance in them that he would actively participate and use them practically in life?

Alvin was right. Had I completely ignored the sociocultural lens that impacted the school in tremendous ways? Had I played school with them, blamed them for not turning in obsolete worksheets, patted myself on the back for trying without actually deconstructing my own literacy teaching and its true impact on my students? Had I not considered the role of out-of-school learning and students' families and communities in my English teaching (Perry, "Knowing")?

◆◆◆

This experience has long impacted my teaching and how I see myself as an English educator. It is important in any space, but particularly in diverse contexts, that students know that the English teacher understands the academic, social, and cultural implications of place and space, expects the best, affirms who they are, works with the community to accomplish learning, and teaches students in ways in which the richness and depth of their new understanding can be best demonstrated and applied. Urban teaching is complex, relational, affirming, and important. The role of English language arts education is no longer to prepare students to read and write in a sterilized, single-skilled environment, but it is to instruct students to meet the literacy challenges of the real world, which requires connecting to humanity and using multiple skills at once to convey a well-crafted message in a complex, multicultural society.

In the United States, 49.1 million students attend public schools. Of this number, 14.4 million—about 30 percent of the public school student population—attend school in urban areas. The population who attends urban schools is comprised of 34.3 percent Hispanic students; 30.3 percent white students; 25.2 percent black students; and 10.2 percent of the students are Asian, Pacific Islander, American Indian, or two or more races (National Center for Education Statistics). Our urban students, significant in number, diversity, and as individuals, deserve the best education—the type of education we give our wealthiest and richest students. To do this, however, we must also recognize, not ignore, the challenges that impact our urban students. Students who live in urban areas experience "economic disparity" in that "over 80 percent of the high-density poverty areas in the United States are located in the nation's 100 largest cities. A disproportionate number of minority students and their families are plagued by this concentration of 'urban poverty'" (Kincheloe 5). In addition, the students face not academic performance gaps but "opportunity gaps" (Boykin and Noguera 22).

Despite the challenges, we know that urban schools are places of resilience, requiring resilient English educators. Preparing an English teacher to instruct culturally diverse students requires *enhanced* preparation—preparation to appreciate the richness of every child's language and the abilities and values of the students' families and communities; preparation to access students' abilities to create, think, and process information in nontraditional ways using culturally relevant teaching and sustaining pedagogies. To do this effectively, English studies education must design programs and opportunities for teacher candidates and practicing teachers that meet the needs of twenty-first century students. Teaching English as isolated, discrete skills with only a Eurocentric focus will not provide any of today's students with the needed skills to function in a richly diverse society, full of multidisciplined and multiliterate opportunities.

Arnetha F. Ball, Richard H. Milner, Ernest Morrell, and Sonia Nieto and Patty Bode all emphasize the importance of English teachers knowing about the community and being familiar with its culture.[1] To prepare today's English teachers, it is not enough to just *know* the English content; it is also important for English teacher candidates to *become involved* and have interaction with the communities that impact students' lives to provide their students with a learning platform to educate the whole child. It is then that English can become a real tool for teachers, a tool for change and authenticity.

The Model of Generative Change (see Ball 46) frames the importance of well-developed, preplanned learning opportunities for teachers as they learn more about teaching diverse learners. According to Ball, generativity is "a teacher's ability to continually add to their understanding by connecting their personal and professional knowledge with the knowledge they gain from their students in order to produce or originate new knowledge that is useful to them in pedagogical problem solving and in meeting the educational needs of their students" (Ball and Tyson 410). This model is a process that uses reflection, metacognition, and generative problem-solving skills to prepare teachers. Teachers use the generative process to create new knowledge and solutions when they encounter challenges in practice. In other words, if we can teach preservice English students to think strategically about *teaching* rather than rely solely on their own preconceived models and practices about language, writing, and literature, then the newly critically constructed knowledge can perpetuate a paradigm shift in how English teachers approach teaching and learning in the classroom and beyond. Together, the critical and generative approaches will be called in this chapter the "generative critical pedagogical approach" to English education. I define this as an explicit, ongoing learning process and additive model that teaches educators to think *critically* about teaching as they question and generate new knowledge based on their research and practice. Critical pedagogy is generative in its own right, but in an English teacher education context, the generative process should be explicit and emphasized, creating ongoing dialogue and processing between and among students and teachers. An example of generative critical pedagogy in action is below.

## Generative Critical Pedagogy in Action: School-Based Literacy Centers[2]

As a result of my experiences with Alvin (the middle school student whose dialogue begins this chapter) and, years later, my English teacher candidates, my students and I developed literacy centers in eight urban high schools, which provided preservice teachers time to work with the students and learn about the community outside of traditional teaching spaces. This work has allowed the organic nature of teaching, learning, and relationship-building to emerge, confronting head-on barriers that can often build division among people when there is limited interaction and conversation. One teacher candidate wrote in her literacy center reflection log:

> Today's [urban] students may be bored with our pre-selected booklists, but they are not bored with reading—to the contrary, they get excited when they discover books they find relevant and interesting. As teachers, it is our job to seize upon this excitement and provide students with the time and resources necessary to foster a true love for reading.

Having an opportunity to work with students directly, learn with them, and participate in their communities outside of the college classroom impacted how teacher candidates interacted with students. As a result, she could begin to challenge the notion that urban students, in particular, do not like reading. She saw them in a different light—as readers—but of the material that captured *their* interests and imaginations.

That's why *knowing* is not enough (Ball 70). Knowing only implies that we have read or have some understanding about a task or skill. But *doing*, the application, the critical review of knowledge and its work in action, is an opportunity to create sustainable generative learning with students, which occurs best when we are an active part of the process as learners ourselves. English teacher candidates must have opportunities not just in college classrooms or even in K–12 classrooms alone but in communities to better understand how to improve learning. If we want culturally responsive, engaging, and curious English teachers, we must provide action-oriented, responsive, generative, problem-solving, resiliency-building opportunities for them to grow, ask questions, challenge their own notions, and develop as advocates and scholars. *Knowing* the skills alone is not enough. *Knowing* the skills and ways of teaching that we treasure without closely examining their worth and application for the next generation is no longer enough, either.

The two following case studies illustrate different frames for considering the role of English studies in English language arts preparation. Each case study is a description of an English language arts teacher's reflection on preparing for the urban classroom and actual teaching experiences. One way to think about each case study is through the lens of generative critical pedagogy, the closing of the "knowing" and "doing" gap. The second lens (since knowing the subject alone is no longer enough) is the four tenets used in the Urban Teacher Enhancement Program (UTEP) that emphasize ways in which we should consider teaching our discipline: affirming attitude, sociocultural competence, pedagogy for diversity, and collaboration, particularly in English education.

## Conceiving the Discipline as a Process: Preparing English Teachers to Teach in a Diverse Context

Developing as conscious, generative critical educators requires teacher candidates and practicing teachers to remain open to understanding students' lives and their experiences (Steinberg; Morrell; Nieto and Bode). When teachers' and students' lives are different culturally, teachers must reach beyond their comfortable safe zones and with awareness step into the world of the student. This is a process of the evolving discipline and its relevance in the twenty-first century. Because the current education workforce consists of 88 percent white, middle-class females who instruct culturally diverse learners (Darling-Hammond), having an enhanced understanding and awareness of diverse students is critical (Lee). To many teacher candidates, the learning of skills and the understanding of culture seem like disconnected ideas and quite frankly, forced, unrelated pedagogies (Delpit). To address the need for a more authentic and responsive teaching, the English education students admitted to UTEP experience a value-added model to integrate components into the program to strengthen their preparation to instruct diverse populations. Although all disciplines are included in the UTEP program, I specifically speak to the discipline of English language arts in English studies.

UTEP (see Voltz et al.) addressed many of the challenges teachers face when instructing K12 students. UTEP historically had been supported by three grants from the US Department of Education, boasting a retention rate of over 90 percent and graduating more than 100 teachers. Many still remain in the teaching workforce. UTEP was a teacher preparation program designed for students who had the knowledge, skills, and dispositions to promote high levels of student achievement in urban schools and who were committed to remaining in those schools.

Working with and placing English teacher candidates in urban school contexts and communities, though, has not been without challenges. In almost twenty years of doing this work as a teacher educator, I can remember two of my students, both white females, as being vehemently opposed to teaching in urban schools for their practicum hours. The first prospective teacher admitted she was afraid to teach in an urban school. Her reluctance was founded in the local nightly news and rumors that circulated in her suburban community, perpetuating fear and despair. The second preservice teacher was so upset at her placement in an urban school that she contacted the department chair and reported it as "punishment" and "personal dislike." This was a deficit view of urban communities and families—the view that placement in an urban English classroom was synonymous with negative consequences. In both instances, though, the students benefitted tremendously from the English education urban teaching experience, learning to deconstruct their own negative thinking about language, race, and class in the urban English classroom. As Bruce McComiskey notes, we must seek difference and think critically about our stance. We must self-interrogate to further expand our knowledge and generate new understandings. But still, this was not enough—a start but not enough.

As one of the university liaisons for UTEP, I was responsible for working with future secondary urban teachers to help them understand how to work with all students. The program was designed to prepare English language arts teachers to work in urban teaching—gaining urban experience in the field, processing new learning and pedagogical skills, integrating the community into teaching, creating assignments that challenged their own positions of power and privilege through language, and selecting responsive materials for students. English language arts majors enrolled in two required classes: the first class created a foundation in teaching English language arts skills using texts, articles, field experiences, lesson planning, and a few community-connecting opportunities; the second one focused more deeply on the application of the learning. To further discuss preparation of ELA teachers for a diverse context, I will share conversations with two UTEP scholars (Kathy and Laura) who graduated from the program, including their thoughts about their preparation in ELA.

## Kathy: Moving from Knowing English to Doing English

Kathy, a young African American female in her thirties, was a third-year urban middle school teacher. She started her career in the business field, but she quickly learned that teaching was the occupation she wanted to pursue after feeling unfulfilled. Leaving her job, Kathy pursued her teaching certificate as she worked in an English education urban classroom. Her school, Stover Middle School, was located in a city school system that had been significantly impacted by the population flight to the suburbs, with only 330 students in the 6–8 school. Kathy taught reading and English in the same fifty-minute class in five sections with a total of ninety students on her roster. The school was 98 percent African American and 78 percent free and reduced lunch. Overall, the income levels for the community members fell between low to middle income, according to the 2010 US Census.

Before we started our conversation, I asked Kathy to rate herself as an English teacher based on the four competencies: affirming attitude, collaboration, sociocultural awareness, and pedagogy for diversity. The areas in which she rated herself the highest were affirming attitude (believing that urban students could achieve at high levels in reading, writing, language, speaking, and listening) and collaboration (working together with teachers and promoting resiliency in herself and with colleagues). Kathy assessed herself lowest in sociocultural competency (lacking a deep understanding of how complex schooling was—a combination of the historical, political, social, and economic influences) and in pedagogy for diversity (use of resources to meet the needs of her students and designing lessons to work more effectively with diverse students).

Kathy started the ELA teacher education program, particularly the methods course, a little apprehensive about pedagogy for diversity—learning styles, adapting traditional lessons, giving options to students for writing, writing workshop approaches, and creating products for learning. She admitted she had in her mind that she wanted to teach the way she was taught in college. Her "mind picture" of the teacher in the front of the room talking and all of the students listening attentively was etched in her psyche as the classroom she would ultimately inherit. She quickly learned, however, that this image was only a dream, and if she wanted to succeed, she would have to adjust her practices.

Kathy learned much from her students. First, she found it unsettling that the students believed they were unable to learn like other children, particularly those in more affluent districts.

The students themselves repeated the educational news stories (based on test scores and discipline reports). The images on television and in movies about urban schools were also damaging to the students' expectations of themselves. Kathy was angered by the onslaught of negativity and wanted to impact positively her students' images of themselves. She began to incorporate different engaging practices in her classroom. She distributed surveys to students to gather information about their interests. Based on this new knowledge, she found that students were very in-tune with their world, particularly popular culture. At that point, she started to design lessons that had real-world relevance, tying to current events, music, and poetry. She also offered students unstructured time to write—to practice their own craft without always being provided a prompt or structure. She also mentioned how society stereotyped her children from a sociocultural standpoint: "Diverse learners are usually pushed to the side. But I know my students can learn anything. I teach them differently. I have to know how they learn best." Kathy acknowledged that she must teach her students "to do English," to use their skills to push back on the stereotypes that try to define who they are.

Collaboration was a part of the school culture. She mentioned that her school colleagues collaborated constantly to manage academic and nonacademic needs of students. "My principal pushes collaboration across the curriculum." In addition to team collaboration, she tried to collaborate with parents as well. One thing that kept her going was that she stayed positive, tried not to fall into a negative slump, but remained realistic. Kathy wrote the following observation in her reflection log:

> Parents play a major role in the lives of students, their attitudes toward school, and the support system for the teacher. Parent involvement looks different today than it did years ago. Parents are working two jobs and at night. It may look as if the parents don't care, but that is rarely the case. I have to find ways to communicate—texting, emailing—that usually work. In today's world, you don't always see the parents at games, recitals, or PTA.

Kathy at first experienced some disappointment with the lack of traditional parental involvement. However, as part of her adaptive practice, she has now transitioned to new language and definitions of parent engagement, honoring ways that parents *do* participate in the lives of their children, such as helping with homework, referring their children to the local tutoring program, arranging college visits in person or virtually—activities that may look different from the old models of parent involvement, which used restrictive language controlled by school, such as attendance at PTA meetings and serving as a room parent. Kathy also now collaborates with the community, finding grants and other resources to assist her students and parents, which is a result of adapting her perspective and language about parenting and schooling.

English studies needs to address more directly and concretely the sociocultural aspect of teaching. Teaching students to use reading and writing as tools for change is important work—relevant and empowering. To include this in English studies for teachers would allow Kathy to see herself as an agent for change in the field, even with approaches to working with families. How do we currently prepare English teachers to "do" English? We specialize in the knowing, but we are weak in the doing.

avoiding deficit - what isn't there

## Laura: Focus on Sociocultural Competence and Pedagogy for Diversity: Changing How We Define "English"

Laura taught in an urban high school with 94 percent African American population and 70 percent free and reduced lunch. Students ranged in ability, from receiving special needs services to collegebound ninth graders. Laura was a second-career teacher from a rural town. She identified as a white, middle-aged woman who decided to enter urban education later in life because of the desire to make a difference in the lives of children who needed her most. She understood this perspective because her own experiences mirrored those of some of her students. Laura wrote this in her reflection log:

> I feel that I can relate to my students at some level. I did not grow up in a large city; I grew up rural, but my home life was very dysfunctional and at times, abusive. I had very little family

> support. Not all urban students experience this, but there are many who live without parents and stay with aunts, cousins, and grandmothers. There are seven siblings in my family. Large family. And I never knew my father. Sometimes people in the community avoided me because they knew my situation. I did not go to college right after high school. I never had anyone to say, "I don't care what your family situation is or what your background is, you can do whatever you put your mind to." It was never any of that motivation or encouragement. And so I know that all of those other things play a role in growing up, but that does not have to define your life and goals.

Laura rated herself extremely high in sociocultural competency. She strongly believed that the social and cultural lenses of a student could not be separated from academic learning. She was alarmed that more of her colleagues did not value the role of culture in teaching English. "They were rarely interested in using the community and resources to impact the teaching and motivate the students." This frustrated Laura.

> So many people don't get it. But I get it because I've been there and done that when I was growing up. And when you are dealing with that crap at home and outside of school, it is very difficult to go to school and turn all that off. A student can't say, "Let me go in here and completely immerse myself in my English classes and worry about learning grammar without thinking about home and other influences." It does not work that way.

To Laura, teaching English was contextual. She understood the wholeness of learning—how the home and school environments impacted each other and how school was not separate from life.

Laura felt as if she had to build a relationship with her students, and part of this relationship building was being "real" with them about who she was. In a class of thirty, for example, Laura taught twenty-eight students who were black and two students who were white. She felt as if she had to talk honestly with the students and address the question, "What does this white woman know about me and my life?" When Laura was talking about literature or writing with students, her own background emerged during the conversations. She described a discussion when the class was reading Cynthia Voight's *Homecoming*. The students were appalled that the mother left her children in the parking lot in the car and never returned. Students then asked Laura how she felt about that cruel act. Laura shared, "I haven't got a clue about my daddy. Never knew him, never met him. . . . I've been on my own since I was fourteen." Students then began to deconstruct their own notions of race, privilege, and power as they reflected on the notion that a white, middle-aged woman would have experienced hardship and disappointment. Laura admits that this impacted the students greatly and made them see her as a person, not just as a preconceived white person. The ever-evolving role of language and learning about the human experience through literature and writing are important in English studies. And the classroom should be a space to have open discourse about these experiences. It is the role of the English teacher to help students navigate these opportunities and teach the students to use their literacy tools for expression, impact, and change.

An affirming attitude added to Laura's success for the year. Even though she had challenges, she remained resilient. "I am constantly looking for things. What can I do—what new text or new activity can I find to reach the students? What can I find to show them they can be anything you want to be and do anything you want to if you believe in yourself, learn from oppressive situations, and use your experience and prior knowledge to help motivate you?" Laura wanted her students to know that she expected much from them, and she tried to use varied texts and lessons that affirmed who they were as young adolescents, engaged them in discussion, and led them to critical ways of thinking about literature and language as well as their own social context.

The community was very supportive of Laura. She actually had an unnamed benefactor who donated individual books and class sets to students for the year totaling over two thousand dollars. "There is something special about having your own book." It also kept Laura encouraged knowing there were other people who believed in the work she was doing and the promise of the children in her classes. "I've never worked so hard in my whole life as I did this past year. The problem is that the textbook, the kids don't relate to it. They were so much more involved and interested when I used novels." Laura benefitted immensely from learning to use young adult literature in the English classroom.

English studies has a gap between what we know and what we do. We know that diverse students need to see themselves in literature, yet we continue to require old, outdated texts as seminal works for students to read. This trickles down to the K–12 classroom. We should actively engage in work that pushes English studies to expand its definition of literature and use texts in our college classes that represent the richness of our national and global cultures.

## Conclusion

Kathy and Laura discussed their teaching experiences and the impact of preparation received in their classes with a focus on English language arts. Based on their experiences, these teacher candidates, now practicing teachers, believed their work in the ELA program added value to their teaching lives in five ways: incorporating high expectations while attending to realities; collaborating with community, parents, and colleagues; making connections with students; confronting stereotypes and generalizations with students; and designing learning for a diverse context.

If we are to prepare our ELA teacher candidates to work in a diverse context, we cannot overlook the importance of any of the themes that emerged from the discussion with the ELA teachers. To meet these demands, we will need to instruct our future teachers to understand the urban context through experiences in urban communities and schools, and to instruct our future teachers to problem-solve to help their students receive the support they need to be successful. Our assignments should maximize their learning and create meaningful opportunities for them to experience the political, economic, social, cultural, and moral issues surrounding urban education. As McComiskey states, the evolution of English studies must advance to meet the challenges and demands of society. To do this, ELA teachers will need to be critically conscious and prepared to instruct every student. ELA teacher education has an opportunity to be at the forefront of this moment. Working with English studies, teacher education programs should provide opportunities for teacher candidates to grow as teachers for all children. As we continue to learn and reflect on our programs, integrating more authentic opportunities for prospective teachers to consciously reflect, learn about, and become authentic members of the larger diverse community is imperative. English studies must close the knowing–doing gap. The existing dichotomy harms students and perpetuates culturally nonresponsive teaching practices. If we know, for example, that students' home language is valuable to the learning process and to the student, we should teach linguistics through an inclusive lens. If we know that culturally diverse students spend their years reading literature that never includes them, never reflects the richness of their cultures, then we must expand the literature and redefine how we select texts. My student Alvin and his classmates deserve it.

## Notes

1. All of these authors write about equity practices for students: Ladson-Billings; Nieto and Bode; Voltz, et al.; Ball and Tyson; Paris and Alim.

2. The following paragraph is an excerpt from Perry's "Generative Critical Pedagogy in English Language Arts Methods for Urban Schools."

## Works Cited

Ball, Arnetha F. "Toward a Theory of Generative Change in Culturally and Linguistically Complex Classrooms." *American Educational Research Journal*, vol. 46, no. 1, 2009, pp. 45–72.

Ball, Arnetha F., and Cynthia A. Tyson. *Studying Diversity in Teacher Education.* Rowman & Littlefield Publishers, 2011.

Boykin, A. Wade, and Pedro Noguera. *Creating the Opportunity to Learn: Moving from Research to Practice to Close the Achievement Gap*. ASCD, 2011.

Darling-Hammond, Linda. *The Flat World and Education: How America's Commitment to Equity Will Determine Our Future*. Teachers College Press, 2010.

Delpit, Lisa. *Other People's Children: Cultural Conflict in the Classroom.* The New Press, 2006.

Freire, Paulo, et al. *Pedagogy of the Oppressed*. Bloomsbury, 2018.

Kinloch, Valerie, editor. *Urban Literacies: Critical Perspectives on Language, Learning, and Community*. Teachers College Press, 2011.

Ladson-Billings, Gloria. *The Dreamkeepers: Successful Teachers of African American Children*. Jossey-Bass, 2009.

Lee, Carol D. *Culture, Literacy & Learning: Taking Bloom in the Midst of the Whirlwind*. Teachers College Press, 2007.

Milner, H. Richard. "Preservice Teachers' Learning about Cultural and Racial Diversity: Implications for Urban Education." *Urban Education*, vol. 41, no. 4, 2006, pp. 343–75.

Morrell, Ernest. "Critical Research and the Future of Literacy Education." *Journal of Adolescent & Adult Literacy*, vol. 53, no. 2, 2009, pp. 96–104.

National Center for Education Statistics (NCES). (2010). *Urban Education in America*. Retrieved May 10, 2013, from http://nces.ed.gov/surveys/urbaned/students.asp.

Nieto, Sonia, and Patty Bode. *Affirming Diversity: the Sociopolitical Context of Multicultural Education*, 7th ed. Pearson, 2018.

Paris, Django, and H. Samy Alim. *Culturally Sustaining Pedagogies: Teaching and Learning for Justice in a Changing World*. Teachers College Press, 2017.

Perry, Tonya B. "Generative Critical Pedagogy in English Language Arts Methods for Urban Schools." *Reclaiming English Language Arts Methods Courses: Critical Issues and Challenges for Teacher Educators in Top-Down Times*, edited by Jory Brass and Alan Webb, Routledge, 2015, pp. 135–46.

———. "Knowing Is Not Enough: The Promise of Community and School-Based Teacher Preparation." *Journal of Language and Literacy Education*, June 2019, https://jolle.coe.uga.edu/wp-content/uploads/2019/06/SSO_June2019_Perry.pdf.

———. "Multiple Literacies and Middle School Students." *Theory Into Practice*, vol. 45, no. 4, 2006, pp. 328–36.

Steinberg, Shirley R. *19 Urban Questions: Teaching in the City*. Lang, 2010.

Voltz, Deborah, Loucretia Collins, Janice Patterson, and Michele Sims. "Preparing Urban Educators for the Twenty-First Century." *Action in Teacher Education*, vol. 29, no. 5–6, 2008, pp. 25–40.

# Index

# EDITOR

**Bruce McComiskey** is a professor of rhetoric and writing and director of the Center for Rhetoric in Society in the English department at Virginia Tech University. His books include *Teaching Composition as a Social Process* (2000), *Gorgias and the New Sophistic Rhetoric* (2002), *Dialectical Rhetoric* (2015), *Post-Truth Rhetoric and Composition* (2017), and *Rhetoric and the Dead Sea Scrolls: Purity, Covenant, and Strategy at Qumran* (2021). He is editor of *English Studies: An Introduction to the Discipline(s)* (2006) and *Microhistories of Composition* (2016) and is coeditor of *City Comp: Identities, Spaces, Practices* (2003).

# Contributors

**Tonya B. Perry** is a professor at the University of Alabama at Birmingham in the School of Education in secondary English language arts. She is the coauthor of *Supporting Students in a Time of Core Standards: English Language Arts, Grades 6–8* (with Rebecca Mannery) and is coauthor of *Teaching for Racial Equity: Becoming Interrupters* (with Steve Zemelman and Katy Smith). She is currently the executive director and principal investigator for the Red Mountain Writing Project and GEAR UP Alabama grant.

**Jacquelyn Rahman** is an associate professor of linguistics at Miami University. She is past director of the Linguistics Program. Her research focuses on topics in social justice with attention to language discrimination and ideological systems that lead to the formation of slurs. Rahman has published numerous book chapters and articles in journals, including *American Speech*, *Journal of English Linguistics*, and *English Worldwide.* She has been interviewed on sociolinguistic issues by various radio and print media sources. Her forthcoming book is *The N Word Papers: Uncovering Secret Messages to Help Heal the Divide.*

**Sarah E. Sandman** has a PhD in rhetoric and composition from Ball State University. She also has experience as a creative writer and editor. She started and runs *The Dandelion Review*, a literary magazine and press for writers on the LGBTQIAA+ spectrum. She teaches writing at Purdue University Fort Wayne and enjoys spending time with her wife and her pets.

**Richard C. Taylor** is an associate professor of English at East Carolina University, where he has served as director of first-year writing and of undergraduate studies in English and has served as graduate advisor and area coordinator for programs in multicultural and transnational literatures, folklore, and film. He is the author of *Goldsmith as Journalist* (1993) and articles on eighteenth-century culture, theater pedagogy, women's studies, and postcolonial literature.

**Victor Villanueva** is Regents Professor Emeritus, a former director of composition, director of a university-wide writing program, director of an American studies program, English department chair (twice!), editor of the Studies in Writing & Rhetoric monograph series of the Conference on College Composition and Communication, former head of that organization, its Exemplar, Rhetorician of the Year, and more honors. With scores of articles, books, and talks on various subjects, he remains most concerned with the interplay of rhetoric and racism.

**Jeffrey J. Williams** writes on contemporary American fiction, the history of modern criticism and theory, and critical university studies. His book *How to Be an Intellectual: Essays on Criticism, Culture* (2014) aims for his version of "public theory." He has also edited the collections *The Critical Pulse: Thirty-Six Credos by Contemporary Critics* (coedited, 2012) and *Critics at Work: Interviews 1993–2003* (2004) among others and published more than 70 interviews with critics, philosophers, and editors. In addition, he is an editor of the *Norton Anthology of Theory and Criticism* (3rd ed., 2018). He is a professor of English and of literary and cultural studies at Carnegie Mellon University.

*This book was typeset in Sabon by Barbara Frazier.*
*Typefaces used on the cover include Balboa and Avenir.*
*The book was printed on 50-lb. White Offset paper*
*by Seaway Printing Company, Inc.*